Your Happy Healthy Pet™

Boston Terrier

2nd Edition

Elaine Waldorf Gewirtz

BICENTENNIAL
1807
WILEY
2007
BICENTENNIAL

Wiley Publishing, Inc.

Copyright © 2007 by Wiley Publishing, Inc., Hoboken, New Jersey. All rights reserved.

Howell Book House
Published by Wiley Publishing, Inc., Hoboken, New Jersey

For general information on our other products and services or to obtain technical support please contact our Customer Care Department within the U.S. at (800) 762-2974, outside the U.S. at (317) 572-3993 or fax (317) 572-4002.

Wiley also publishes its books in a variety of electronic formats. Some content that appears in print may not be available in electronic books. For more information about Wiley products, please visit our web site at www.wiley.com.

Library of Congress Cataloging-in-Publication Data:
Gewirtz, Elaine Waldorf.
    Boston terrier / Elaine Waldorf Gewirtz. — 2nd ed.
        p. cm. — (Your happy healthy pet)
    ISBN-13: 978-0-471-74818-2 (cloth)
    ISBN-10: 0-471-74818-8
    I. Title. II. Series.
    SF429.B7G49 2007
    636.755—dc22

                                2006024897

Printed in the United States of America
10 9 8 7 6 5 4 3 2 1
2nd Edition

Book design by Melissa Auciello-Brogan
Cover design by Michael J. Freeland
Illustrations in chapter 9 by Shelley Norris and Karl Brandt
Book production by Wiley Publishing, Inc. Composition Services

About the Author

Elaine Waldorf Gewirtz is the author of *Pugs For Dummies, Your Yorkshire Terrier's Life, The Dog Sourcebook, Dogs, The American Pit Bull Terrier, Your Happy Healthy Pet: Miniature Schnauzer,* and *Your Happy Healthy Pet: Chihuahua.* She has also written numerous magazine articles about dogs. She's also a multiple winner of the Dog Writers' Association of America's Maxwell Award for Excellence, and the recipient of the ASPCA Special Writing Award.

Elaine is a member of the Dog Writers' Association of America, the American Society of Journalists and Authors, and the Independent Writers of Southern California. She breeds and shows Dalmatians in conformation and has lived with several breeds all her life.

She dedicates this book to her parents, Leo and Rosalie Waldorf, her sister, Beverlee Jo Waldorf, and the first Bostons, Boots, Debbie, and Scamp.

About Howell Book House

Since 1961, Howell Book House has been America's premier publisher of pet books. We're dedicated to companion animals and the people who love them, and our books reflect that commitment. Our stable of authors—training experts, veterinarians, breeders, and other authorities—is second to none. And we've won more Maxwell Awards from the Dog Writers Association of America than any other publisher.

As we head toward the half-century mark, we're more committed than ever to providing new and innovative books, along with the classics our readers have grown to love. This year, we're launching several exciting new initiatives, including redesigning the Howell Book House logo and revamping our biggest pet series, Your Happy Healthy Pet™, with bold new covers and updated content. From bringing home a new puppy to competing in advanced equestrian events, Howell has the titles that keep animal lovers coming back again and again.

Contents

Shopping List

You'll need to do a bit of stocking-up before you bring your new dog or puppy home. Below is a basic list of some must-have supplies. For more detailed information on the selection of each item below, consult chapter 5. For specific guidance on what grooming tools you'll need, review chapter 7.

- ☐ Stainless steel food dish
- ☐ Stainless steel water dish
- ☐ Dog food
- ☐ Leash
- ☐ Collar
- ☐ Crate
- ☐ Crate bedding

- ☐ Nail clippers
- ☐ Grooming tools
- ☐ Chew toys
- ☐ Toys
- ☐ Flea, tick, and heartworm preventives
- ☐ Toothbrush and toothpaste
- ☐ ID tag or microchipping

There are likely to be a few other items that you're dying to pick up before bringing your dog home. Use the following blanks to note any additional items you'll be shopping for.

- ☐ _____
- ☐ _____
- ☐ _____
- ☐ _____
- ☐ _____
- ☐ _____
- ☐ _____
- ☐ _____
- ☐ _____
- ☐ _____
- ☐ _____

Pet Sitter's Guide

We can be reached at (___)_____-_____ Cell phone (___)_____-_____

_____

We will return on _____ (date) at _____ (approximate time)

Dog's Name _____

Breed, age, and sex _____

Spayed or neutered? _____

Date last heartworm preventive given _____

Date last flea and tick preventive given _____

Important Names and Numbers

Vet's Name _____ Phone (___)_____-_____

Address _____

Emergency Vet's Name _____ Phone (___)_____-_____

Address _____

Poison Control _____ (or call vet first)

Other individual to contact in case of emergency _____

_____

Care Instructions

In the following three blanks let the sitter know what to feed, how much, and when; when the dog should go out; when to give treats

Morning _____

Afternoon _____

Evening _____

Water instructions _____

Exercise instructions _____

Medications needed (dosage and schedule) _____

_____

Any special medical conditions _____

_____

Grooming instructions _____

_____

My dog's favorite playtime activities, quirks, and other tips_____

_____

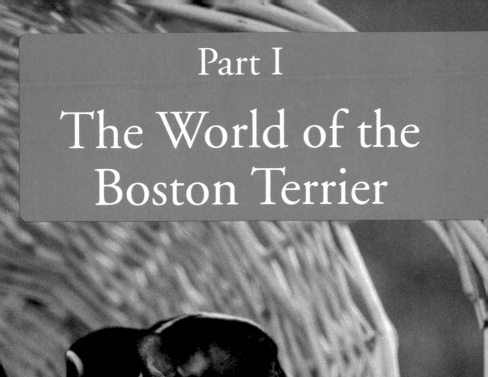

Part I
The World of the Boston Terrier

The Boston Terrier

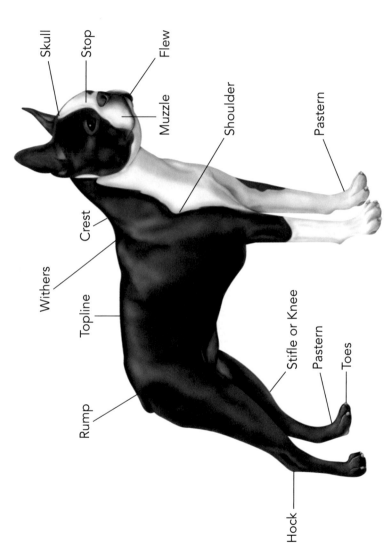

Skull

Stop

Flew

Muzzle

Shoulder

Pastern

Crest

Withers

Topline

Rump

Stifle or Knee

Pastern

Toes

Hock

Chapter 1

What Is a Boston Terrier?

A Boston Terrier is everyone's favorite prom date. Dressed to the nines in a black and white tuxedo, he is quite the dog. With manners galore, this Yankee Doodle boy is outgoing and lively without ever being pushy or snooty. All that's missing is the carnation boutonnière and a stretch limo.

The Boston's nickname is the American Gentleman, and it's a fitting description. Although descended from grand old English stock, he's a true all-American canine success story. The Boston is one of only a few breeds developed in the United States.

The Boston Terrier is friendly and lively, affectionate, loyal, and intelligent. He's a good watchdog and is good with children. He sheds very little, and needs minimal grooming and moderate exercise. In fact, the only special care you must take is that he needs to be kept cool outdoors in warm weather.

It's no wonder that the Boston Terrier placed either first and second in American Kennel Club (AKC) registration statistics from 1905 to 1939, and has always ranked in the top twenty among all breeds registered with the AKC.

A Non-Sporting Breed

The Boston Terrier is a member of the Non-Sporting Group. The Non-Sporting Group is one of seven groups of breeds (the others are Sporting, Hound, Working, Terriers, Toys, and Herding) set up by the AKC. The dogs in each group share similar characteristics, such as their appearance, history, personality, and what job they were originally bred to perform for their owners. Dogs in the

What Is the AKC?

The American Kennel Club (AKC) is the oldest and largest pure-bred dog registry in the United States. Its main function is to record the pedigrees of dogs of the breeds it recognizes. While AKC registration papers are a guarantee that a dog is pure-bred, they are absolutely not a guarantee of the quality of the dog—as the AKC itself will tell you.

The AKC makes the rules for all the canine sporting events it sanctions and approves judges for those events. It is also involved in various public education programs and legislative efforts regarding dog ownership. More recently, the AKC has helped establish a foundation to study canine health issues and a program to register microchip numbers for companion animal owners. The AKC has no individual members—its members are national and local breed clubs and clubs dedicated to various competitive sports.

Non-Sporting group are diverse, perform a variety of tasks, and are generally not regarded as game hunters.

While you might think at first that the Boston Terrier should belong to the Terrier Group because of his name, he technically isn't a terrier. You can learn more about the Boston's ancestry in chapter 2, but the "terrier" part of his name comes from the fact that the Boston was the result of breeding a Bulldog to the now-extinct White English Terrier.

Careful, selective breeding over the years produced a dog with a body that is more like a terrier's than a Bulldog's, although Bostons inherited their friendliness toward people from the Bulldog.

The Ideal Boston

The ideal Boston Terrier is probably sitting on your lap right now. To many pet owners it doesn't matter what their Boston's ears look like or how long his body is, as long as he doesn't run out of kisses for everyone in the family and is healthy and active.

Conscientious breeders think these characteristics are first and foremost, but they work very hard to raise the bar. There are many small dogs who are good looking, sweet, and fun-loving, but it's the Boston Terrier's head and his distinctive tuxedo markings that set him apart from all other breeds.

This chapter briefly describes the Boston Terrier's breed characteristics, as outlined in the breed standard. To read the official breed standard, refer to the web sites of the AKC or the Boston Terrier Club of America (listed in the appendix).

Size

The AKC breed standard divides Bostons into three weight classes for show purposes: under 15 pounds, 15 pounds to under 20 pounds, and from 20 to 25 pounds. According to the standard, you should be able to tell the difference between males and females just by looking at their overall size; the females should also look slightly more refined.

Although the standard doesn't mention how tall Bostons should be or how much males and females should weigh, breeders generally produce females who weigh 12 to 14 pounds, and males who range between 15 and 18 pounds. Breeders like to see Bostons no taller than 12 inches at the top point of the shoulder (called the withers) and no shorter than 9 inches.

Bostons come in a few sizes, but all are definitely small.

Neck, Topline, and Body

The Boston's body is small, compact, and square, not spindly or coarse. The head and neck help balance the dog, so the neck should be just the right length, slightly arched, and in balance with the head.

If the dog's tail curves upward, it's a fault, and it's a serious fault if it is ever docked (cut to make it shorter). It's a serious fault if the Boston has a sway back (sags in the middle), a roach back (an upward curvature of the spine), or is slab-sided (flat ribs without much spring to create a rounded appearance).

The Boston's back should look short; just short enough to square the body.

Head

The Boston's breed standard has 100 points, with each feature of the dog assigned a certain number of those points. Because the Boston's head sets him apart from all other breeds and is an important characteristic, 15 points are assigned to the head.

Like his overall appearance, the Boston's head should be square and in proportion to the rest of the body. A Boston with a correct head can take your breath away. The head should be free from wrinkles, and have flat cheeks with a well-defined stop. (The stop is the indentation where the nose joins the skull.) The expression should be alert and kind, which indicates intelligence.

His square, well-proportioned head sets this breed apart.

Eyes

Look into a Boston's eyes and you will see his soul. His eyes should be set wide apart, and be round and dark. The eyes should not show too much white or haw, which is the third eyelid. Blue eyes or any trace of blue disqualifies a Boston in the show ring. There are very few Bostons with blue eyes because responsible breeders never use dogs with blue eyes for breeding. Veterinary researchers have suggested that there is a slight correlation between blue eyes and deafness.

What Is a Breed Standard?

A breed standard is a detailed description of the perfect dog of that breed. Breeders use the standard as a guide in their breeding programs, and judges use it to evaluate the dogs in conformation shows. The standard is written by the national breed club, using guidelines established by the registry that recognizes the breed (such as the AKC or UKC).

The first section of the breed standard gives a brief overview of the breed's history. Then it describes the dog's general appearance and size as an adult. Next is a detailed description of the head and neck, then the back and body, and the front and rear legs. The standard then describes the ideal coat and how the dog should be presented in the show ring. It also lists all acceptable colors, patterns, and markings. Then there's a section on how the dog moves, called *gait*. Finally, there's a general description of the dog's temperament.

Each section also lists characteristics that are considered to be faults or disqualifications in the conformation ring. Superficial faults in appearance are often what distinguish a pet-quality dog from a show- or competition-quality dog. However, some faults affect the way a dog moves or his overall health. And faults in temperament are serious business.

Ears

The ears are small and erect, and should be as close to the corners of the head as possible. They can either be cropped or left natural. The desired effect is for the ears to stand erect.

When a puppy is teething, between 12 and 18 weeks of age, his ears will frequently be a little floppy and stick out slightly from the side. They settle into their permanent position by about 8 months old.

When they are finished teething, many Bostons have ears that naturally stand erect. When they don't, some breeders will have them cropped, which means surgically removing the extra piece of earflap that prevents them from standing erect. Many breeders can tell early on what the ears will look like when the dog is full grown. They may use tape to reinforce the soft cartilage in the ear if it is folded over.

Cropping is controversial and is prohibited in Britain, New Zealand, and some other countries. If you want a Boston with perfect ears and want to have them cropped, this procedure must be done when he is just a few months old. Only a very experienced veterinarian who specializes in this procedure should perform this surgery. Before proceeding, discuss cropping thoroughly with your dog's breeder and your veterinarian. There is a great deal of care required after the surgery.

No matter what position your Boston's ears eventually assume, he will always be a wonderful pet for your family.

Muzzle and Nose

The Boston's muzzle is short and must be proportionate to the skull. It should be free from wrinkles and shorter than it is wide or deep. From the stop to the end of the nose, the muzzle is parallel to the top of the skull.

The nose should be black with a well-defined line between the nostrils. If a dog has a Dudley nose, he's disqualified from competing in the show ring. (A Dudley nose is a flesh-colored nose without any black pigmentation; it is more susceptible to sunburn.)

When a Boston's mouth is closed, his tongue and teeth should not be showing. If so, it's a serious fault in conformation competition.

Color and Markings

Three colors are mentioned in the Boston Terrier breed standard—brindle, seal, and black—all with white markings. Brindle is a pattern in which layers of black hairs in regions of a lighter color produce irregular stripes. Seal is black with a red cast when viewed in the sun or

The cute, scrunchy muzzle and upturned nose are important for maximum adorableness.

bright light. According to the breed standard, brindle and white is the preferred Boston color, but a black and white coat is permissible.

Solid black, solid brindle, or solid seal without white markings is a disqualification. The Boston must have a white muzzle band, a white blaze between the eyes, and white on his forechest.

There is no such thing as a Boston of a rare color such as red, blue, or all white. Sometimes unscrupulous breeders or brokers will try to sell dogs of these colors for a very high price and say they are rare and special Bostons. But they absolutely are not Bostons, no matter what they tell you. Here's why: A Boston is a Boston because he's brindle, seal, or black, with white markings. That's what the breed standard says, and the standard is what defines the breed. So buyer beware!

Gait

The Boston Terrier does not have a job that requires specific athletic ability, such as running after game or chasing down a fox. His main job is to be a treasured companion. Nevertheless, it's still important that the Boston's gait be sure-footed and that he move with perfect rhythm, with each step showing grace and power.

It's a fault if the dog weaves, rolls, or paddles his feet when he trots. It's a serious fault if one foot crosses in front of the other while the dog is moving. The idea here is that the Boston's movement should be straight and efficient without being cumbersome.

Temperament

The breed standard says that the Boston's disposition should be friendly and lively. Of course, you probably already knew that!

Chapter 2

Boston Terrier History

One look at the Boston Terrier, and it's easy to imagine an artist dipping his brush first into black, then into white, to hand paint the world's very first Boston. Surely the breed's smooth, clean contrast is there by deliberate design.

She is, after all, an original breed—named after the city of her origin. Unlike other breeds whose history is hazy and obscure, passed down by word of mouth, much of what we know about the Boston Terrier is well-documented. This tuxedo-clad dog is as American as the Boston Tea Party, so it's hard to believe that her ancestors lacked the same blueblood family tree.

The First Boston Terrier

The distinguished American Gentleman you see today is actually descended from a mongrel named Judge, who was a cross between an English Bulldog and a now-extinct White English Terrier. Judge's relatives weren't American. Judge was imported from England by Bostonian William O'Brien and purchased in 1865 by Robert C. Hooper, also a Boston resident. To identify their new companions in those days, owners named their dogs after themselves, so Judge was known as Hooper's Judge.

It was an uncertain period in American history. The Women's Suffrage Movement had begun, the Civil War was over, and President Abraham Lincoln was assassinated. It was also a time when many wealthy people imported dogs from Europe because they missed the dogs of their former homes, who had been reliable workmates.

In those days, dogs were bred to perform a specific job, such as guarding, herding, hunting, or fighting. Butchers used the bull breeds to control bulls brought to them for slaughtering. Soon the popular sport of bull baiting was born, in which bulls were tethered to a strong stake and a Bulldog or a bull-and-terrier mix was assigned the task of using her strong jaws to pin a bull to the ground by grabbing onto its nose.

Bull baiting required a dog who was powerful, courageous, and tenacious. While Bulldogs fit the description, they lacked the speed and animation that attracted an excited betting crowd. So breeders of bull-baiting dogs began breeding their Bulldogs to the athletic and spirited terrier breeds.

Historians believe Hooper's Judge was specifically imported as a fighting dog. He looked nothing at all like the Boston Terrier of today. He was tall and weighed about 32 pounds. Old records show that Judge was a dark brindle with a white blaze and throat and a screw tail, although they do not tell us who his parents were.

Another surprise was that Judge's offspring had none of the aggressive qualities of his ancestors, the fighting dogs. His descendants were very companionable with sweet, loving personalities, so it's no wonder that the Boston Terrier was dubbed the American Gentleman because of his spirited but gentle disposition.

Judge was bred to Mr. Burnett's stocky white female, Gyp, probably imported from Liverpool. This breeding likely produced several puppies, but

Although her distant ancestors were English, the Boston Terrier is all American.

the puppy described in the records as being the next in line in the Boston Terrier's development was Well's Eph. This puppy grew up to be a dark brindle dog with even markings, not as tall as his sire and weighing about 28 pounds.

Eph was bred to Tobin's Kate, a golden-brindle bitch who weighed about 20 pounds and was fairly short, with a blocky head and a longer, straighter tail. We don't have any pedigree records on these dogs, but they were presumably either imported from Liverpool or descended from dogs imported from Liverpool. Eph and Kate's litter was whelped in 1877, and included Barnard's Tom, who was owned by John P. Barnard.

Historians consider Tom to be the first Boston Terrier and the true foundation of the breed. He weighed about 22 pounds and had a red brindle coat with white on his forehead, collar, chest, and feet. He had the typical screw tail we see today. Tom still probably resembled the Pit Bull or Staffordshire Terrier type, but he was closer to what we think of as a Boston.

Records show that Tom was bred to a female named Kelley's Nell. Apparently, Barnard took the pick of the litter as Tom's stud fee. That puppy, named Mike, is recorded as the first of these dogs to truly resemble the modern Boston Terrier. He was a light brindle with white markings, had the full, round eyes favored today, and weighed about 25 pounds. His body resembled the Staffordshire Terrier, and his flat face and screw tail suggested his Bulldog ancestors.

Early Colors and Markings

Most of the early dogs were brindle with white markings. However, a few were mostly white, including Gyp. Gyp's great-grandson, Sullivan's Punch (Mike's son), and his daughter, Ch. Lady Dainty, were examples of white Boston Terriers who were considered excellent examples of the breed despite their color.

Today breeders occasionally produce puppies who are primarily white with some brindle markings. Although this pattern is less desirable, these dogs are as nice as their brindle-and-white or black-and-white littermates (who are not primarily white). The standard for the breed does not say "preponderance of white on the body" is a disqualification, or even a fault. It is merely a "deficiency"; and if a white Boston possesses "sufficient merit otherwise," she could compete in conformation. However, most modern-day breeders do not show or breed white dogs.

Boston's First Dog Show

The first dog show held in Boston was in 1878, and several of these early dogs, then called Bull Terriers, competed. By 1888, the Boston dog show provided a class for "round-headed bull terriers, any color," the designation for this breed at that time. Barnard (owner of the famous Tom and Mike) judged that class at the show.

Originally, brindle with white was the most popular color combination.

The name caught on, and for awhile the breed was popularly called Round Head or Boston Round Head. At about the same time, the name Boston Bull also became popular, although it might have referred to either the round-headed dogs or the brindle Bull Terrier, also developed in Boston. This nickname, although never part of the official name of the breed, remains in common use today, with many people incorrectly calling the breed Boston Bull Terrier.

A Breed and a Club

In 1890, thirty Boston Terrier breeders from the Boston area formed a club and called themselves the American Bull Terrier Club. This club sought formal recognition from the AKC in 1891, but the AKC denied their application because the breed was not sufficiently well established at that time. The Bull Terrier and Bulldog breeders didn't like the club's name, either, because they felt that it also referred to their dogs and that the Boston, with her short head and body, was so different from these breeds.

In honor of its city of origin, the club changed the breed's name to Boston Terrier, and the Boston Terrier Club of America (BTCA) was admitted into AKC membership in 1893. It was the first purely American breed to have AKC recognition, and the BTCA became one of AKC's oldest member clubs. The

The Boston has some terrier characteristics and some Bulldog qualities.

AKC stud book certified seventy-five dogs whose ancestors could be traced back three generations to purebred Bostons.

The breed was first registered in Canada in 1888, and the first Boston to become an AKC champion was Topsy, at the Philadelphia Dog Show in April of 1896. The second champion, a dog named Spider, came a year later.

Not a Terrier

Is the Boston Terrier a terrier? No. The name was retained because the breed was bred down from bull-and-terrier crosses. Bostons inherited their friendliness toward people from the Bulldog, but the body is more terrierlike. She has some Bulldog qualities and some terrier qualities. Plus she has some qualities that are all her own.

Although some people mistakenly call the breed a Boston Bull or a Toy Bulldog, early Boston Terrier breeders worked tirelessly to establish type—those qualities that make the Boston Terrier unique and the breed you see today. In the process, the breed has become a smaller and more compact dog than her ancestors.

Toy Bostons?

Over the years, changes in weight classes developed, and for a few decades, very small Bostons, weighing less than 10 pounds, were known as Toy Boston Terriers. Although some Bostons are this small today, this size is considered too tiny for safe breeding and good health, and conscientious and responsible breeders spay or neuter these Bostons. Most Bostons who are shown at dog shows today range from 12 to 25 pounds.

A Popular Dog

By the early part of the twentieth century, the Boston's sweet, easygoing nature and her small but sturdy size easily made her one of the most popular breeds in the United States. It only took twelve years for the Boston to become the

The Boston Terrier Breed Club

If you like Boston Terriers and want to learn more about the breed, consider joining the national breed club, the Boston Terrier Club of America (BTCA). BTCA members have been responsible for developing and improving the breed for more than one hundred years. They wrote the original breed standard, under AKC guidelines, and the club is responsible for maintaining or revising it as needed.

The BTCA is the parent organization of regional Boston clubs throughout the United States. Both the BTCA and the regional clubs encourage and promote quality breeding of purebred Boston Terriers, sponsor dog shows under AKC rules, and promote sportsmanship in competition.

For more information about applying for membership, contact the BTCA (see the appendix). You'll be joining a dedicated group of Boston breeders and owners whose main purpose is to preserve the Boston's heritage.

nation's most popular breed. From 1905 to 1939, she took turns placing either first or second in AKC-ranked registration statistics. The breed remained ranked among the top ten most popular breeds in the AKC through 1963—the only breed at that time to hold that distinction.

By the mid-1960s, the breed's popularity declined somewhat, until she was remembered again in 1976, when she was named America's Bicentennial Dog and Massachusetts named her the official state dog.

Lately there is renewed interest in this dapper dog. New owners are rediscovering the breed and realizing that she is not merely the old dog their grandmothers once had. Bostons are springing up on television and in print advertisements alongside the latest aspirin, room freshener, flea preventive, carpet cleaner, and dog food.

In 2005, the Boston Terrier ranked seventeenth among all breeds registered by the AKC, with 15,852 dogs registered. It looks as if the Yankee Doodle Dog is once again beloved in the country of her birth.

Chapter 3

Why Choose a Boston?

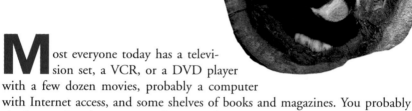

Most everyone today has a television set, a VCR, or a DVD player with a few dozen movies, probably a computer with Internet access, and some shelves of books and magazines. You probably also have a CD player, a case of CDs, and maybe a digital camera, a cell phone, and an iPod.

With so many ways to spend your free time at home, why, then, do you want a dog? And why this breed?

Why Do You Like Boston Terriers?

Is it his striking good looks? Does his small, compact body and short hair speak volumes to you? What about the fact that he doesn't need weekly trips to the groomer to look his best? Do you have your heart set on a dog with an intelligent demeanor who is always eager to entertain you with his antics?

There's also his Bulldog and terrier heritage to consider. Although Bostons have some of the same genetic combinations as the American Pit Bull Terrier and other fighting breeds, they took a detour sixty years ago to a kinder, gentler personality. Specifically bred to be companions, their personalities range from a mellow, more determined Bulldog, to a feistier here-I-am terrier attitude. Is this the kind of temperament you want to spend the next thirteen years with?

One of the best reasons to have a Boston Terrier is his temperament. Enthusiastic, yet rambunctious, even-tempered, yet intellectual, here's a big dog in a little body. He loves nothing better than to be the center of the household.

If you're still unsure if a Boston is your canine soul mate, contact the nearest Boston Terrier club and talk to other Boston owners. Ask them to tell you about their dogs and what it's like to live with one. Spend time visiting Boston breeders to determine what they like and don't like about the breed.

Smarty Pants

There's no question that Boston Terriers are extremely intelligent dogs who learn quickly. If you say to a well-trained Boston, "Go get the ball, not the rope toy, and it's in the bedroom and not in the den," he will follow your directions exactly. Here's a breed who understands not only everything you say, but also watches your every move like a hawk. This means that when it comes time to discussing your dog's birthday present with another family member, you'll have to write your ideas down. Otherwise, the dog will know what you're planning for him just by listening. Scary, huh?

Tuxedo-clad dogs are naturally curious, too. They love to explore new places and follow their noses through fields and woods. Although they don't have the same reputation for scenting ability as Bloodhounds and Beagles, they're smart enough to learn to use their noses, and some have even earned AKC tracking titles.

Bostons excel at obedience trials and are serious competitors. They understand exactly what they need to do with agility obstacles and, when trained well, will focus on their trainer. Bostons are more than willing to follow directions without trying to reinvent the wheel and do things their own way, which is always a bonus.

Because they are easy to train, Bostons do well in a wide variety of organized sports, including agility.

A Cool Companion

The Boston Terrier has been bred for more than 100 years to be a household companion. This is his job and it's what he does best. He should be eager to accompany his humans on outings and be a good ambassador, happily greeting one and all. The ideal Boston Terrier has never met a stranger. He greets everyone as a friend. He expects every human to offer kind words, a gentle pat, or perhaps a special treat. Every other dog is a potential ally and playmate.

Boston Terriers are people dogs. They love following their families around from room to room and doing whatever they're doing. If you're watching television, your dog will be content to sit beside you and catch up on the latest episode. Cooking in the kitchen? Count on your Boston to watch you chop veggies, hoping for a sample.

Sized Right

Many people appreciate the Boston's small size. About 12 inches tall at the withers (measured from the ground to the top of the shoulders) and weighing less than 25 pounds, he doesn't take up much room in the car if you're going for a drive. He's easy to take for a walk, doesn't eat that much, and best of all, is a great lap dog and loves to cuddle.

As long as he gets enough exercise, a Boston can live comfortably in an apartment. If he's lucky enough to have a big house with a securely fenced-in yard, he'll like that, too.

Bostons don't take up much space.

If you're hoping to move your new Boston into an apartment or a rental home, check with your landlord first. Many apartment and condo complexes don't allow dogs or only permit small dogs (such as Bostons). If they do give you the go-ahead to bring your dog, be prepared to pay extra for this privilege. Many landlords require an extra deposit and charge an additional cleaning fee if you have a dog. They're also not very tolerant if your Boston barks a lot and the neighbors complain.

Come vacation time, many people like to take their dogs traveling with them. As long as the weather is cool, Boston Terriers are great traveling buddies. They're interested in all things new and different, and adapt easily to new circumstances. If you're going on a road trip, remember not to leave your dog locked in the car during the daytime and even on some warm evenings. Inside a closed car, the temperature can shoot up dangerously high.

> **TIP**
>
> Remember that Bostons overheat quickly when the weather is warm, so walk your dog either early in the morning or late in the day when the temperature cools down.

Exercise

Like people, all dogs need some exercise to stay in good health. It stimulates the respiratory and circulatory systems and keeps them fit. Your Boston doesn't need to have a large house and yard to be healthy; a small yard will do, especially if you take him out walking. In fact, you don't need a yard at all. Going for a walk at least once a day, chasing a ball or retrieving a stuffed animal inside your home prevents boredom, loneliness, and stress.

The exercise you choose for your dog should suit his age and overall physical condition. A young Boston tires faster than a mature dog will, and seniors need to take it slow. When you begin an exercise program with your dog, start slowly and gradually add more time. And remember, he's never going to be able to walk as fast or as far as you can.

Bostons love to play tug of war with a rope toy, either with another dog or with you. Although it's tempting to satisfy this feisty urge, resist! If you pull the rope too hard, you can loosen your dog's teeth. This also isn't a good game for a dog who already thinks he's king of the world. When he wins the rope he thinks he's in charge, which he's not. You are.

A Long Life Ahead

Bostons are hardy dogs, especially when they are fed a healthy diet, have regular exercise, and receive quality medical care. Give your dog a loving environment and responsible training and you can look forward to having him with you for ten to thirteen years or more. Of course, every dog is different and genetic illnesses can take their toll on a dog's health (see chapter 8 for more information), but giving your dog all the right stuff is the best insurance you have.

The Dog's Senses

The dog's eyes are designed so that he can see well in relative darkness, has excellent peripheral vision, and is very good at tracking moving objects—all skills that are important to a carnivore. Dogs also have good depth perception. Those advantages come at a price, though: Dogs are nearsighted and are slow to change the focus of their vision. It's a myth that dogs are color-blind. However, while they can see some (but not all) colors, their eyes were designed to most clearly perceive subtle shades of gray—an advantage when they are hunting in low light.

Dogs have about six times fewer taste buds on their tongue than humans do. They can taste sweet, sour, bitter, and salty tastes, but with so few taste buds it's likely that their sense of taste is not very refined.

A dog's ears can swivel independently, like radar dishes, to pick up sounds and pinpoint their location. Dogs can locate a sound in $\frac{6}{100}$ of a second and hear sound four times farther away than we can (which is why there is no reason to yell at your dog). They can also hear sounds at far higher pitches than we can.

In their first few days of life, puppies primarily use their sense of touch to navigate their world. Whiskers on the face, above the eyes, and below the jaws are sensitive enough to detect changes in airflow. Dogs also have touch-sensitive nerve endings all over their bodies, including on their paws.

Smell may be a dog's most remarkable sense. Dogs have about 220 million scent receptors in their nose, compared to about 5 million in humans, and a large part of the canine brain is devoted to interpreting scent. Not only can dogs smell scents that are very faint, but they can also accurately distinguish between those scents. In other words, when you smell a pot of spaghetti sauce cooking, your dog probably smells tomatoes and onions and garlic and oregano and whatever else is in the pot.

Built-in Alarm System

Chances are you won't need to have an expensive home alarm service if you have a Boston Terrier. This is an alert breed who feels very protective of his environment. His hearing is acute, and when someone comes to the door his bark is sharp and menacing. Burglars will think twice before entering your home without permission and running the risk of tangling with your dog.

Generally, Bostons won't bark unless they have something to say, but you can train your dog to stop barking. If you want to encourage your dog's watchdog tendencies, reward him for barking when strangers come to the door but discourage him from barking nonstop.

Why Not a Boston?

Although it's hard to imagine anyone not wanting an all-American playmate, there are a few things you should know about the Boston Terrier before you run out and get one. Nothing is worse than acquiring a dog and later realizing that he's not the one for you. Once you take him home, he's yours for the next dozen or so years. So make sure this is the dog you really want.

Bostons can sometimes be a handful. This is not a passive canine who sits idly by waiting for you to make decisions for him. This is a breed who thinks for himself and has every intention of pleasing his owners—as long as it fits into his own plan.

He Wants to Be with You

There's no ignoring a Boston. Don't leave him alone outdoors for long periods of time, because he won't like it. Besides, a Boston is a family pet, not some creature you ignore all the time. Of course if there's no one at home during the day, your dog will have to be left alone, but he'll need companionship when you come home.

Before you decide to add a dog to your family, give some serious thought to how you like to spend your free time. If you often work late during the week and can't wait to get away from home on the weekend, your Boston isn't going to appreciate being shipped off to a kennel or left with a pet sitter all the time. Will you be spending long weekends taking the kids to their year-round sports activities? Feeding your dog breakfast and then leaving him alone for long hours, day in and day out, is no life for a Boston Terrier—or any dog. When you finally do manage to spend some quality time with him, don't be surprised if he begins acting out, often becoming destructive and annoying, just trying to keep your attention before you run out again.

Your Boston Terrier will want to be with you all the time.

Weather Warnings

Dark coats and short muzzles make Bostons vulnerable to heatstroke on warm days. Even on a balmy spring day, the temperature in the sun or in a car can quickly become uncomfortable and quite dangerous for a Boston. When in doubt about the temperature, don't take your dog for an outing without knowing if there is shade available if you need it. If not, pack a shade awning or a beach umbrella.

When you have a Boston, you need to recognize and be able to treat the beginning symptoms of heatstroke (see chapter 8 for more information). Be sure to bring plenty of cool water and a small towel or a chamois, which you can use to cool off your dog. Wet it down thoroughly and hold it up against your dog's armpits, stomach area, and groin. He'll cool off much faster this way than if you were to place a wet towel on top of him.

Being a small dog and having short hair means Bostons are also more vulnerable in very cold temperatures. Their sensitivity varies, with some Bostons loving cold weather and snow, and others trembling and making a beeline for the warm dog bed in the house. If you're planning to take your Boston out in cold weather for more than a couple of minutes, put a coat or a sweater on him. This keeps him warm by holding in his natural body heat. You'll find plenty of adorable dog sweaters and coats in pet supply stores, doggy catalogs, and on the Internet. With such wonderful accessories available, there's no need to make winter outings unpleasant for your little friend.

Noisy Nose, Messy Mouth

Yes, Boston Terriers are noisy and messy. You can blame their flat faces and short muzzles for the snoring, noisy mouth breathing, and foamy nostrils and saliva. If you want a Boston, get used to it. With any luck, you won't hear the sound of sawing logs after a few months and will stop noticing the foam. Until then, there isn't much you can do about it anyway, except to buy some earplugs and to stock up on facial tissue.

Other Dogs

The Boston Terrier is descended from tough, ferocious dogs: Bulldogs and terrier crosses. Bulldogs were developed to work with butchers to engage and control cattle—animals who were many times their own size and who could cause fatal injury if the dog was not quick or tough enough. The terriers who contributed their genes to the Boston's family pool were fighting dogs—fearlessly fighting their own kind but completely harmless to humans. Throughout the generations, Bostons were selected as much for their easygoing, nonaggressive nature as for their type and structure.

Bostons can be aggressive toward other dogs, particularly when they are behind a fence or on a leash. This may be something the dog has learned, or it may be a genetic tendency. Regardless of its origins, don't think that this behavior is acceptable.

Buying an adorable sweater for your dog is about as fun as shopping gets.

You can change this behavior by teaching the dog to focus on you and by rewarding him with praise and treats for ignoring the other dog or dogs. Under no circumstances should a dog be punished or corrected for this aggressive behavior by yanking on the leash, yelling at the dog, or hitting him. The aggressive behavior is usually caused by fear, and punishment can increase the fear and thereby increase the aggression.

Don't hesitate to contact a professional dog trainer or an animal behaviorist if you need help training your dog.

Chapter 4

Choosing Your Boston Terrier

Now that you've selected the breed you want, it's time to choose your next canine American Idol. Will it be a cute and cuddly puppy or an older and, hopefully, wiser adult? Do you prefer those white markings on a brindle, seal, or black background? Having any Boston Terrier may sound good to you, but since this dog is a lifetime commitment and will be with you for ten to thirteen years, your job is to choose the best one for your home and lifestyle. How do you do that?

Begin by finding out as much as you can about the behavior, care, and training of puppies and adult dogs. Then listen to your heart and be truthful to yourself about what you can or cannot do. The next stage is finding the best breeder or locating a good rescue organization or shelter. Whatever you do, don't rush the elimination rounds and take the first dog you meet. Finding a solid gold dog and breeder takes time and patience, and when you cast your final vote you'll know which Boston is the right dog for you.

Puppy or Adult?

Can't decide if you want a puppy or an older dog? Give some serious thought to how much dog experience, time, money, and patience each of them will require. Puppies and adults have different needs. Evaluate the pros and cons of each before running out and buying or adopting the first adorable Boston you see who gives you a smooch.

Love Pup

If you're leaning toward a puppy, you'll have to housetrain her during the first few weeks, and take her outside in the middle of the night to eliminate. You'll also have to keep your possessions off the floor so she doesn't chew them up. Then there's crate training, and for the first few months, feeding her three times a day. She'll also need exercise and other outings to meet and greet strangers to help socialize her.

Caring for a puppy is almost like having a second job, plus it can be very expensive. Purebred puppies from quality breeders can cost $1,000 or even more. Then there are supplies to buy, and the cost of veterinary care.

Some people prefer a puppy because they can train her themselves and build their own bond early on. Or they want to know the breeder and their puppy's sire and dam, see how the pup spent her early days, and be able to watch her grow up. If you've thought about these responsibilities and still want a puppy, then a pup is the right choice for you.

A Full-Grown Boston

If you think you don't want to go through the housetraining or the silly chewing stage, but don't want an adult Boston because you think she's too old to be any fun, guess again. A Boston may be considered an adult when she's a year old, but she'll carry on her Boston Terrier hijinks for many years to come.

Puppies have their charms, but so do adult Bostons.

There are other advantages to having an adult. She's probably already been housetrained and somewhat socialized, you can see what size she is when fully grown, she only needs to be fed twice a day, and you will see her adult temperament and personality. An older dog may not cost as much to buy or adopt, and she's had most of her vaccines. Don't worry that your adult won't bond with you, either. Once a Boston gets to know you, she's your best friend forever.

On the flip side, a grown dog may have a few bad habits that you'll need to correct. Although it's hard to imagine, many Bostons are abandoned by their owners because they no longer want to take care of a dog or because the dog might have behavior issues (which can be overcome with patient training).

Male or Female?

Both male and female Boston Terriers are sweet and loving, and you'll be happy with either sex. It's just a matter of personal preference. However, there are a few differences between them. With a male reaching puberty there may be a few embarrassing moments when he mounts your leg or a friend's. He also has the need to mark his territory by lifting his leg and urinating against odd objects, such as your best coffee table, the barbecue, a chair, or the stairway railing. He thinks he's in charge of the household. Taking him to obedience classes and having him neutered should prevent those behaviors from reoccurring.

Some people think males are more affectionate than females, but that's really an individual trait and is not linked to sex. Other Boston owners believe females are quieter and aren't as playful as males, but again, each dog is different.

If you already have a dog and are planning to get another, your best choice is to get one of the opposite sex. Two females together will have a greater tendency to argue, and even fight one another. Two males together will also pick fights with one another.

Where Should You Get Your Boston Terrier?

There are many sources for dogs and puppies, and some are better than others. Begin by contacting the Boston Terrier Club of America (BTCA). The club can help you find a local Boston Terrier club and can give you the names of breeders in your area.

Reputable Breeders

There are many people who may call themselves breeders, but not all breeders are created equal. Conscientious, reputable breeders care about the welfare of their breed and breed dogs solely to improve the quality of the breed. They test the quality of their stock by showing their dogs and competing in canine sports. Even if you don't want a show dog, buying from a breeder of this caliber gives you a better chance of having a good pet. All of the pups in such a litter, whether they are destined for the show ring or are pet quality, are raised the same way and have show quality or champion parents.

The reputable breeder is usually a member of the Boston Terrier Club of America, a regional Boston club, and perhaps a local dog club. This person studies pedigrees, plans litters sometimes years in advance, and knows a great deal about the behavior, care, health, and training of Bostons.

Reputable breeders test their dogs for any genetic weaknesses before they breed them to make sure that they don't pass on any health problems to their offspring. They do not raise puppies as a source of income. Since many Bostons must have their puppies delivered by Cesarean section, and litters often have only one to four puppies, many breeders lose money by breeding. They also spend whatever it takes to care for the mother and puppies.

Reputable breeders carefully plan every litter to breed the soundest puppies possible.

Reputable breeders raise their puppies at home, with plenty of socialization and love.

When you visit breeders, you can see the conditions the pups were raised in, the dam and sire (or a photo of him), and perhaps other relatives. They will give you a hint about how your pup may look and act when she grows up.

How is the mother dog? Does she look healthy? Is she friendly and outgoing, welcoming you in to see her pups? A mother Boston who is wary of strangers or overly protective of her babies may be teaching the puppies to be wary. Lessons learned at this young age from her mother or her breeder will stay with your dog for a very long time.

Bostons are house dogs and should be kept indoors in the family home. Puppies raised in kennels, barns, garages, basements, or cages, away from family life and activities, may have difficulty adapting to their new homes. Puppies who grow up for the first eight or ten weeks as part of a family will make better family pets.

When you buy a puppy from a conscientious breeder, you are also buying that breeder's expertise. She will always welcome any questions you have about health, care, behavior, and training.

Be prepared for the breeder to interview you. She wants to make sure you will take very good care of the pups she worked so hard to bring into this world. Some of the questions she'll ask will deal with how much experience you have with dogs, where you plan to keep your dog, and why you want a Boston Terrier.

Commercial Backyard Breeders

There are other breeders who raise puppies solely as a source of income. No thought is given to the pedigree or if the sire and dam are free from genetic weaknesses or are well suited to one another. If there's no pedigree, you have no way of knowing if the father is even a purebred Boston Terrier! If you ask to see proof of health tests, these breeders may or may not have them. Many commercial backyard breeders do not want to spend the time or money for health tests and will say that their dogs don't need to be tested because they already know they are healthy. But there is no way to know whether a healthy dog carries a deadly gene, except by testing.

These breeders do not actively show their dogs, so their quality has never been proven. Without incentives to breed the best quality Bostons, they will sell pups to anyone who can write a check. They don't screen buyers and won't be responsible for their dogs later on if there's ever a problem.

Be wary of these breeders. Ask how many litters they have each year. Quality breeders can't have more than a few each year. When litters are raised properly, there's only so much time available for personal care of the pups. And it's so important for puppies to be well socialized during their first few weeks of life, because otherwise they grow up frightened or aggressive.

Pet Stores and Brokers

A reputable breeder never sells puppies to a pet store or to any other third party such as a broker, because she won't know anything about the new owner and whether the puppy will have a good home. While a reputable breeder is always responsible for the puppy if she's no longer wanted later on, that's not the case with a pet store or a broker—once they make a sale, it's final. A pet store will never take a dog back and will not answer your questions months or years later, the way a breeder will.

While some pet stores do offer health guarantees, not all do. And the guarantee is often limited to a short time period. These stores get their pups from commercial breeders, who breed for volume and profit, not health and temperament. The sire and dam are not usually checked for genetic problems, and the pups are not raised in a home environment.

Online Sales

The Internet can be a great source of information about dogs, but you have to be a careful consumer. Go online and you'll see hundreds of web sites listing Boston Terriers. Some of these belong to reputable show breeders and others are set up by commercial backyard breeders. How can you distinguish the reputable breeders' web sites from the commercial backyard breeders' sites?

Conscientious breeders usually only breed Bostons, because one breed takes years to breed well. Commercial backyard breeders often have several different breeds available. Conscientious breeders will also ask you to call them before they will discuss selling any pups, while all you have to do to get a pup from a backyard breeder is to type in your credit card information. They'll happily ship you a puppy if you live far away, or they will agree to meet you somewhere.

If there are photos and names of the sires and dams of the puppies, a reputable breeder's site shows that they are AKC champions. Backyard breeder sites may not have AKC-registered dogs, so you can't prove if the pups are purebred or not (the AKC requires all males who sire more than a few litters to be DNA-tested for proof of identity).

Selecting Your Puppy

After you've interviewed breeders, it's time to choose your puppy. Study the breed standard so you can appreciate the excellent qualities the puppies have. Ask the breeder to explain anything in the standard that isn't clear to you.

If more than one puppy is available, plan to visit more than once to get a better idea of the individual personalities in the litter. If possible, take your whole

Every Boston you meet will be appealing in her own way.

Signs of a Healthy Puppy

Look for a healthy puppy with these characteristics:

- The eyes should be clear without any discharge or redness.
- The puppy should be active and not huddled in a corner or lying down most of the time.
- The coat should be sleek and shiny, not thin, patchy, or dry.
- The puppy should not be itchy or have dry, flaky skin.
- The puppy should be eager to greet you and want to crawl into your lap.
- The puppy should have a healthy appetite.
- The puppy should not have diarrhea or be vomiting.

family to visit the puppies. Everyone will be responsible for caring for the puppy, so they might as well share in the choice. Besides, it's fun to see puppies! Just don't fall in love with all of them or even with the very first pup you see.

Watch the whole litter to get an idea about their individual personalities. Puppies should be healthy and outgoing, eager to interact with other siblings and visitors. Shy puppies sitting off in the corner will require more socialization to come out of their shells, and will need careful supervision if there are small children in your home.

How Old Should the Puppy Be?

Puppies go through some critical developmental stages and should be kept with their littermates until they are at least 8 weeks old. Many breeders even prefer to keep Boston puppies until they are 12 to 16 weeks of age. During this early time, puppies learn from their mothers about proper doggy behavior, social interactions, and body language. This education continues in your home, where your puppy will learn from you about how to interact properly with humans and other pets.

Puppies separated from their mothers and littermates before the age of 8 weeks may display more fear of new things, including other dogs, and can become aggressive.

Getting the Right Papers

When a breeder tells you that the dog she is selling comes "with papers," be prepared to do some reading. She is referring to a big notebook filled with a lot of information about your dog. Many conscientious show breeders will also give you photographs of your dog's ancestors and some tips about care and feeding your new Boston. Carefully review these papers before agreeing to buy any dog.

A Pedigree

When you purchase your Boston, the breeder should give you a copy of your dog's three-generation pedigree, which is your dog's family tree. The top of the pedigree shows the sire's relatives, and the bottom shows the dam's. There is no guarantee that your dog will look or act exactly like her relatives.

Historically, Boston breeders and owners named their dogs by including their own names in the registered name, such as Hooper's Judge, who was owned by Robert C. Hooper in 1865. Today, breeders choose a distinctive name for their kennels and incorporate that when they select a registered name for a dog. Therefore, on a pedigree you'll likely see the same first name (the kennel name) in a few of the ancestors.

The AKC Application for Registration

The breeder should give you the AKC application to register your dog. Only the breeder can obtain this form, after she has registered the litter of puppies with the AKC. To complete your dog's registration, you'll need to fill in your dog's name and send this form, with the required fee, to the AKC. The AKC will register your dog and send you a registration certificate with your dog's identification number. Your dog is now recorded in your name and you are the owner.

Beware of a seller who tells you the application for registration will be along later. She should have all the papers ready when she is ready to sell the pups.

Health Records

You should receive a list of the vaccines your Boston has received with the dates they were given, and when your dog has been wormed. The breeder should also give you a copy of your Boston's BAER hearing test, which can be done at 5 to 6 weeks of age. The results of a preliminary patella (kneecap) examination by a veterinarian should also be given to you, although the patellas cannot be certified until the dog is at least 1 year old.

A puppy younger than 8 weeks is too young to leave her mom and littermates. Some breeders hold on to puppies even longer.

Copies of the sire's and dam's eye examinations and certification from the Canine Eye Registration Foundation (CERF) should also be included. When your puppy is 8 weeks old, the breeder should have her eyes examined by a canine ophthalmologist for the presence or absence of any congenital eye defects, and those results should be given to you. You'll still need to have your dog's eyes examined yearly, because the eyes can change.

The Contract

You should also receive a bill of sale from the breeder. It should include the puppy's name, the names of the puppy's sire and dam, the date of birth, her sex, color, the date of the sale, and the price you paid.

It should include the breeder's requirement that the Boston be spayed or neutered, and that you will take the dog to the veterinarian within twenty-four to forty-eight hours. This will let you know that you have purchased a healthy dog. The bill of sale also specifies the terms necessary to receive a refund if you later decide that you want to return the dog.

Most important is the breeder's health guarantee. While no breeder has a crystal ball to see if there are any genetic problems in the puppies they produce, reputable breeders try their best to breed out genetic problems by testing their breeding stock for any genetic problems and diseases before they breed them. Of course, there's no guarantee that a dog won't develop a fault or a disease later on in life.

Still some breeders will guarantee that the dog will be free of genetic problems and will return part of your original purchase price or give you another dog if yours develops a disabling genetic defect by a certain age.

Adopting a Rescued Boston

There's no shortage of Bostons to adopt. Contact the Boston Terrier Club of America, which has a rescue coordinator. There are other Boston rescue organizations you can find online who have dogs who desperately need new homes.

Expect the dog you adopt from a rescue group to be spayed or neutered and to be current on vaccinations. She should have been kept in foster care long enough to determine whether she is housetrained, crate trained, and leash trained. Her temperament should also be evaluated. If you have other pets in your home, the rescue group should offer you a Boston who has been tested and has been found to be friendly to the pets you have.

Part II

Caring for Your
Boston Terrier

Chapter 5

Getting Ready for Your Boston Terrier

At long last you've found the Boston Terrier of your dreams and it's almost time to bring your Yankee Doodle Dog home. The first few days will be exciting, that's for sure, so keep your camera batteries charged so you can capture all of those early magic moments.

You'll have years of adventures with your new best friend to look forward to. But first there are a few things you need to do to help your all-American buddy feel right at home.

Boston-Proofing

Whether you're bringing home a puppy or an adult Boston Terrier, your home and outdoor areas need to be dog-proof. Your dog doesn't understand that chewing the wrong thing can cause life-threatening intestinal blockage and that you'll be upset with him for destroying your possessions. The box on page 48 gives you a list of things to do before the big day.

A huge yard isn't necessary for a Boston, but the area he does have should be securely fenced and the gates should have strong locks that won't open accidentally. Periodically check the fence and the gates and fix any holes, so that your brave fellow can't slink through.

Boston-proof the rest of your yard by identifying the plants. Many are poisonous if your dog decides to chomp on them. The Department of Animal Science at Cornell University has an extensive list of poisonous plants at www.ansci.cornell.edu/plants.

Your yard should also have a shady area where your Boston can cool off on a warm day. Trees or a covered patio area will do the trick. The breed's flat face and short muzzle make breathing more difficult, especially when it's hot out, so take special care.

Indoors, put treasured possessions out of your dog's reach (and bite) or use baby gates for those rooms that are off-limits. Children's toys are particularly appealing to dogs and need to be kept away from your Boston.

Basic Supplies

A fun part of getting a new dog is going shopping for supplies. The box on page 51 gives you a list of things your dog will need. Be sure to bring your wallet, but don't buy the first squeaky toy you see. Pet supplies are expensive, so shop around for the best deals.

There's no shortage of places to shop for your dog, either. Today dog stuff is sold practically everywhere: discount and pet supply stores, pet boutiques, dog catalogs, and the Internet. The American Pet Products Manufacturers Association (APPMA) reports that sales of pet supplies and medicine have doubled since 1994. In 2004, pet owners in the United States spent $8.8 billion on pet supplies and medicine.

Collar, Leash, and ID

Don't let your Boston leave home without them. He needs a collar and an identification tag for his collar, right when you pick him up. The ID tag should be firmly attached to his collar and have your name, address, and phone number clearly printed on it. When you choose a name for him, you can have another tag printed up with that information. Be sure to have him microchipped later on. (A microchip is a permanent identification device about the size of a grain of rice that your veterinarian can painlessly insert into your dog's body. Veterinarians and shelters

Your dog will need a collar and a leash. Make sure you choose colors that complement his natural good looks.

Puppy-Proofing Your Home

You can prevent much of the destruction puppies can cause and keep your new dog safe by looking at your home and yard from a dog's point of view. Get down on all fours and look around. Do you see loose electrical wires, cords dangling from the blinds, or chewy shoes on the floor? Your pup will see them too!

In the kitchen:

- Put all knives and other utensils away in drawers.
- Get a trash can with a tight-fitting lid.
- Put all household cleaners in cupboards that close securely; consider using childproof latches on the cabinet doors.

In the bathroom:

- Keep all household cleaners, medicines, vitamins, shampoos, bath products, perfumes, makeup, nail polish remover, and other personal products in cupboards that close securely; consider using childproof latches on the cabinet doors.
- Get a trash can with a tight-fitting lid.
- Don't use toilet bowl cleaners that release chemicals into the bowl every time you flush.
- Keep the toilet bowl lid down.
- Throw away potpourri and any solid air fresheners.

In the bedroom:

- Securely put away all potentially dangerous items, including medicines and medicine containers, vitamins and supplements, perfumes, and makeup.
- Put all your jewelry, barrettes, and hairpins in secure boxes.
- Pick up all socks, shoes, and other chewables.

In the rest of the house:

- Tape up or cover electrical cords; consider childproof covers for unused outlets.
- Knot or tie up any dangling cords from curtains, blinds, and the telephone.
- Securely put away all potentially dangerous items, including medicines and medicine containers, vitamins and supplements, cigarettes, cigars, pipes and pipe tobacco, pens, pencils, felt-tip markers, craft and sewing supplies, and laundry products.
- Put all houseplants out of reach.
- Move breakable items off low tables and shelves.
- Pick up all chewable items, including television and electronics remote controls, cell phones, shoes, socks, slippers and sandals, food, dishes, cups and utensils, toys, books and magazines, and anything else that can be chewed on.

In the garage:

- Store all gardening supplies and pool chemicals out of reach of the dog.
- Store all antifreeze, oil, and other car fluids securely, and clean up any spills by hosing them down for at least ten minutes.
- Put all dangerous substances on high shelves or in cupboards that close securely; consider using childproof latches on the cabinet doors.
- Pick up and put away all tools.
- Sweep the floor for nails and other small, sharp items.

In the yard:

- Put the gardening tools away after each use.
- Make sure the kids put away their toys when they're finished playing.
- Keep the pool covered or otherwise restrict your pup's access to it when you're not there to supervise.
- Secure the cords on backyard lights and other appliances.
- Inspect your fence thoroughly. If there are any gaps or holes in the fence, fix them.
- Make sure you have no toxic plants in the garden.

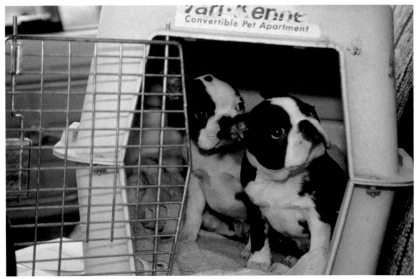

A crate is your dog's safe haven—and your indispensable training tool.

have hand-held scanners that quickly read the ID, so you can be notified if your dog is missing.)

To buy the right size collar before you pick him up, ask your dog's breeder or rescue coordinator what size will fit. Or you can stop at the pet supply store with him on the way home and try a few on to see what fits. If you have a puppy, buy the size that fits now, instead of a collar that's too big, thinking your dog will grow into it.

Buy a sturdy leather leash. If it stays out of your dog's mouth, it will last forever. *Do not* buy or use a retractable leash! While it may look like a fun way to walk your dog, it can also be deadly. If your dog is ten feet away from you and a menacing loose dog suddenly runs up to him, you can't reel him in and protect him fast enough. The line can also slice through your hands or bare legs if you grab at it or it quickly gets jerked against your leg.

The Magic Crate

If you've never used a crate before, it may seem as if you are punishing your dog. But a crate is really a very safe, cozy spot for him when he's sleeping, working on his housetraining skills, or misbehaving and needs a time out. Your Boston should be in a crate for the ride home, because it's safer than riding in a car without any restraint.

Boston Terrier Essentials

You'll need to go shopping *before* you bring your puppy home. There are many, many adorable and tempting items at pet supply stores, but these are the basics.

- **Food and water dishes.** Look for bowls that are wide and low or weighted in the bottom so they will be harder to tip over. Stainless steel bowls are a good choice because they are easy to clean (plastic never gets completely clean) and almost impossible to break. Avoid bowls that place the food and water side by side in one unit—it's too easy for your dog to get his water dirty that way.
- **Leash.** A six-foot leather leash will be easy on your hands and very strong.
- **Collar.** Start with a nylon buckle collar. For a perfect fit, you should be able to insert two fingers between the collar and your pup's neck. Your dog will need larger collars as he grows up.
- **Crate.** Choose a sturdy crate that is easy to clean and large enough for your puppy to stand up, turn around, and lie down in.
- **Nail cutters.** Get a good, sharp pair that are the appropriate size for the nails you will be cutting. Your dog's breeder or veterinarian can give you some guidance here.
- **Grooming tools.** Different kinds of dogs need different kinds of grooming tools. See chapter 7 for advice on what to buy.
- **Chew toys.** Dogs *must* chew, especially puppies. Make sure you get things that won't break or crumble off in little bits, which the dog can choke on. Very hard plastic bones are a good choice. Dogs love rawhide bones, too, but pieces of the rawhide can get caught in your dog's throat, so they should only be allowed when you are there to supervise.
- **Toys.** Watch for sharp edges and unsafe items such as plastic eyes that can be swallowed. Many toys come with squeakers, which dogs can also tear out and swallow. All dogs will eventually destroy their toys; as each toy is torn apart, replace it with a new one.

There are many styles and sizes to choose from, so ask your dog's breeder to recommend the right size. Collapsible wire models are great to use in warm weather because air circulates through and keeps your Boston one cool cat. You can always throw a sheet over the top of it if your air conditioning is on and

TIP

If you'd rather not use a crate for your dog in the car, consider buying a doggy booster seat. The seat attaches to the car seat belt, has a harness that fits over his shoulders, and is high enough that it lets your dog see out the window safely. If you're ever in a car accident, your Boston is well-protected from being thrown out of the car.

you're worried that your dog might be too cold. You can also buy a fitted cover to use all year.

For cold weather, the hard or soft-sided types provide the most protection for your dog. If you're taking your dog on an airplane, the airlines will only allow him to ride in a hard-sided crate or in a carry-on bag that's airline approved.

The crate will need some bedding inside to make it soft and comfy. Don't buy expensive dog cushions until you know whether your dog is a bed chewer. In the beginning, you can line the crate with old blankets or towels that are easy to wash if he has a bathroom accident. Inside, put a soft stuffed animal (without any parts that your dog can chew off and swallow) and a few dog toys. Toss a food treat inside the crate whenever you want your dog to go in, and he'll always like being in there.

Baby Gates

You can probably hold off buying a baby or doggy gate for a few days, but it will come in handy in a few weeks when your dog becomes more adventuresome. Use it to block off a room that's off-limits to your dog or if you need to keep him confined at night.

Gates can be temporary or permanent and you can easily attach them to doorframes or walls. You'll find many types in all sizes at baby stores or in pet supply stores. Choose a model that's easy to use and lightweight enough to move from room to room. If your dog is a chewer, consider buying a metal gate instead of wood or plastic.

Bringing Your Boston Home

Now that you have all the essential supplies your dog will need, it's time to pick up your Boston Terrier. Ask the breeder or rescue coordinator not to feed your dog breakfast on the day of his departure. Don't worry! He won't starve. Some dogs get carsick, so the less food in his stomach, the better.

Your puppy should be at least 8 weeks of age, although many breeders prefer to wait until pups are between 12 and 16 weeks and they've had enough time to bond with their siblings. Show breeders also like to wait a little longer to see whether a pup is a show ring prospect.

The First 24 Hours

Choose a day to pick up your Boston when you can arrange to stay home with him for the rest of the day and perhaps the next. Early morning is the best time. This gives your dog a chance to bond with you and to feel comfortable in his new digs before bedtime. You're probably eager to begin showing him off to your friends and neighbors, but hold off for a few days. To your dog, everything is new, scary, and exciting all at the same time. Let him settle in and begin bonding to you and learning the routine without additional stimulation.

Wait a few hours before you feed him for the first time, so that he has a chance to become accustomed to his new environment. Don't expect your dog to eat all of his first meal. Some dogs need a little more time than others to adapt to their new surroundings.

Hold off doing everything you've always wanted to do with a dog on the first day. Don't show him all of the toys you bought, either. You don't want to confuse your dog with too many options. You'll have your dog for many years to come and can always do something else another day.

Your new pup does not need free run of the house. Temporary gates will keep him safe and out of trouble while he is learning how to behave.

When you go shopping, don't forget to get some chew toys. Puppies absolutely must chew, so give them something safe and fun to destroy.

Set up a regular schedule for your dog to eat, go to the bathroom, play, and sleep. Sticking to a routine, within an hour or two, helps him learn what to expect and how to behave. When you think your dog needs to go to the bathroom, take him outdoors to begin housetraining (see chapter 10 for a complete housetraining program).

Expect your Boston's first night home to be a short one. It's going to take him a few nights to feel confident about sleeping in his new digs. Put a big stuffed animal in his crate with him at night so he has something to snuggle up against for company. If he whines during the night, he may have to go outside. Try not to talk to him too much. It's hard, I know, but resist. Otherwise he'll think that you're rewarding him for waking you. Hopefully, he'll go to the bathroom and then go right back to sleep. You can dream, anyway.

Chapter 6

Feeding Your Boston Terrier

Walk into any pet supply store and you'll see a variety of dog foods available for dogs of all ages, sizes, and shapes. Rows of shelves are stacked with bags and cans. With so many choices, it's no wonder many people feel overwhelmed.

Your Boston Terrier depends on you to provide proper, balanced nutrition. A healthy diet contributes immeasurably to the good health of your dog. How can you tell which dog food is best for your Boston Terrier? If only she could do a taste test in the middle of the store. Since that's not possible, choose a food that provides a well-balanced diet. It should contain proteins, carbohydrates, fats, vitamins, and minerals. Dog food labels should say "nutritionally complete" or "complete and balanced." This means that they meet the minimum nutritional requirements for adult dogs, as established by the Association of American Feed Control Officials (AAFCO). In addition, dogs below the age of 1 year should eat a diet that is specifically formulated for puppies.

Much research has been done about the balance of nutrients, vitamins, and minerals needed to maintain good health in dogs. Nutritional deficiencies or overloads may cause serious health problems. For example, dietary imbalances in protein, calcium, and phosphorus can affect a puppy's growth and development, leading to painful debilitation. Proper nutrition ensures that the dog's body gets all of the building blocks, in the right proportion, that she needs for growth and maintenance.

Feeding dogs is not a simple matter of opening a bag or can and filling a bowl. Every dog has different nutritional needs, and each thrives on a somewhat different combination of foods. Like people, some Bostons have a higher metabolism, or level of energy, and they burn more calories, meaning they need to eat more to keep their weight at the ideal level. Others need a lower-calorie diet because they tend to put on weight. Some dogs enjoy excellent health on a diet that includes a variety of protein sources and grains, while others require a more limited diet because of food allergies or sensitivities.

The more you know about dog food and feeding options, the healthier your dog will be.

So Many Choices

The options available for feeding a dog today are almost as numerous as the number of dogs. There are hundreds of brands of commercial dog food, but all come in one of three basic types: dry, canned, and semimoist. Within these types, there are different formulas for puppies, adult dogs, active dogs, older dogs, big dogs, small dogs, and dogs with different coat types.

You will also find foods developed to meet the dietary needs of dogs with specific health conditions, such as allergies, heart problems, kidney problems, digestive problems, and cancer. You also have the option of creating your own diet for your dog by offering her fresh foods.

No matter what your dog's situation, there is now a food made just for her.

Commercial Dog Food

The majority of dog owners in the United States today feed their dogs commercial dog food, whether it's dry kibble, canned, or semimoist formulas. Each has its advantages and drawbacks. What is best for your Boston?

Commercial dog food varies greatly in quality and nutritional value. In selecting a commercial diet for your dog, you should learn to read the dog food labels (see the box on page 58) and understand the major ingredients. The manufacturers of commercial pet foods follow guidelines that outline what is and isn't permitted to be included in pet food, and how those ingredients can be described on the label.

Look for indications of higher quality. Ingredients listed as lamb, chicken, beef, or turkey mean meat of that specific species is included in the food. Terms such as "meat," "meat by-products," or "meat meal" suggest that various species may be included, and these may not be the healthiest sources of protein for your Boston Terrier. A label that lists human-grade or USDA-approved ingredients is an indication of higher quality in a dog food.

Dry Dog Food

Dry kibble is the most economical form of dog food. The moisture has been removed, so you aren't paying for water. If you do feed kibble, be sure to provide plenty of fresh, clean water for your dog to drink. Add warm water to the food and you can stir in a little low-fat yogurt or cottage cheese.

One of the disadvantages of using dry kibble is that it has a limited shelf life. Unless preservatives are added to the food or to the ingredients used in the food, it will tend to spoil, becoming rancid or moldy. The preservatives most commonly used in animal foods are the chemicals BHA, BHT, and ethoxyquin. As pet-owning consumers have become more vocal in their concern over the use of these chemicals, many manufacturers have replaced them with natural antioxidants, such as vitamin E

The best quality dog food costs a little more, but you feed your dog much less. You pick up after her less, too.

Reading Dog Food Labels

Dog food labels are not always easy to read, but if you know what to look for they can tell you a lot about what your dog is eating.

- The label should have a statement saying the dog food meets or exceeds the American Association of Feed Control Officials (AAFCO) nutritional guidelines. If the dog food doesn't meet AAFCO guidelines, it can't be considered complete and balanced, and can cause nutritional deficiencies.
- The guaranteed analysis lists the minimum percentages of crude protein and crude fat and the maximum percentages of crude fiber and water. AAFCO requires a minimum of 18 percent crude protein for adult dogs and 22 percent crude protein for puppies on a dry matter basis (that means with the water removed; canned foods should have more protein because they have more water). Dog food must also have a minimum of 5 percent crude fat for adults and 8 percent crude fat for puppies.
- The ingredients list the most common item in the food first, and so on until you get to the least common item, which is listed last.
- Look for a dog food that lists an animal protein source first, such as chicken or poultry meal, beef or beef byproducts, and that has other protein sources listed among the top five ingredients. That's because a food that lists chicken, wheat, wheat gluten, corn, and wheat fiber as the first five ingredients has more chicken than wheat, but may not have more chicken than all the grain products put together.
- Other ingredients may include a carbohydrate source, fat, vitamins and minerals, preservatives, fiber, and sometimes other additives purported to be healthy.
- Some grocery store brands may add artificial colors, sugar, and fillers—all of which should be avoided.

(sometimes called tocopherols in its various forms) and vitamin C. While these replacements are all-natural, they do increase the manufacturing cost. Also, their shelf life is shorter. The end result is a higher-priced dog food.

Look for a top-quality dry food because it is more concentrated and you don't have to feed as much. In the long run, it's actually less expensive. It also has ingredients that are easy to digest and you'll have fewer stools to pick up.

Canned Dog Food

Canned food is another option in feeding a commercial diet. The first ingredient in this type of food is almost always water—nearly 75 percent. It also contains meat and vegetable ingredients. Because of all the water, it's not a good idea to give your dog only canned food. It also has no crunch factor, so it lodges in dental crevices and stick to your dog's teeth, which leads to tooth decay. Canned food is more expensive, too, because in order to provide sufficient nutrition, you must feed your dog more of it than you would kibble. You also have to keep it refrigerated once the can is opened, so taking it for your dog when you're traveling isn't always convenient.

> **TIP**
>
> Expect to pay more for healthier foods. You will get what you pay for, and you'll see improved health and vigor in your Boston if you spend a little more for higher-quality foods with fresher, whole ingredients and fewer chemicals.

Semimoist Dog Food

Semimoist foods are popular with some dog owners because of the convenience and the appealing appearance and texture. The semimoist texture is created by adding propylene glycol, which is a sugar that stays soft at room temperature. This chemical also acts as a preservative to increase the shelf life of the food.

Semimoist food also tends to contain more chemical dyes than other types of dog food, because dyes are used to create the different colors of the pieces of food, or to simulate the appearance of fresh hamburger.

We know how excess sugar and food dyes affect humans. These ingredients can have a similar effect on dogs, increasing their excitability. Eating lots of sugar can also cause weight gain and tooth decay in dogs, just as it does in humans.

Supplementing Commercial Diets

If you're thinking about adding supplements to your Boston's diet, first discuss it with your veterinarian. Too many supplements can lead to health problems. Besides, if you select a top-quality food, supplements aren't usually necessary. Everything your Boston needs is already contained in the food.

Different Foods for Different Ages

In looking at the variety of commercial dog foods, you will see that different formulas are available for puppies, adult dogs, high-energy or hard-working dogs, overweight dogs, and older dogs. Puppies are burning a lot of calories just in

Pet Food vs. People Food

Many of the foods we eat are excellent sources of nutrients—after all, we do just fine on them. But dogs, just like us, need the right combination of meat and other ingredients for a complete and balanced diet, and a bowl of meat doesn't provide that. In the wild, dogs eat the fur, skin, bones, and guts of their prey, and even the contents of the stomach.

This doesn't mean your dog can't eat what you eat. A little meat, dairy, bread, some fruits, or vegetables as a treat are great. Fresh foods have natural enzymes that processed foods don't have. Just remember, we're talking about the same food you eat, not the gristly, greasy leftovers you would normally toss in the trash. Stay away from sugar, too, and remember that chocolate is toxic to dogs.

If you want to share your food with your dog, be sure the total amount you give her each day doesn't make up more than 15 percent of her diet, and that the rest of what you feed her is a top-quality complete and balanced dog food. (More people food could upset the balance of nutrients in the commercial food.)

Can your dog eat an entirely homemade diet? Certainly, if you are willing to work at it. Any homemade diet will have to be carefully balanced, with all the right nutrients in just the right amounts. It requires a lot of research to make a proper homemade diet, but it can be done. It's best to work with a veterinary nutritionist.

growing and tend to need more calories relative to their size than adult dogs do. They also need more protein and fat, for growth. Dogs who compete in sporting events, such as obedience, agility, and flyball, may also need more calories per day than normal adult dogs.

Older dogs usually need fewer calories. Some people also believe that older dogs need lower protein levels than younger dogs, but this has proven not to be the case. Older Bostons who are in good health, with normal results on blood tests, can and should eat the same food as younger adult dogs (although probably in smaller amounts). Reduced protein diets may be appropriate for dogs with impaired kidney function, as diagnosed by a veterinarian, but such diets are not necessarily appropriate for older dogs who are basically healthy.

> **TIP**
>
> All dogs will benefit from snacks and treats of fresh fruits and vegetables, rather than dog biscuits or meaty treats.

If you are feeding commercial food, select a brand that uses high-quality ingredients first; then select the variety that is appropriate for your puppy, adult, or elderly Boston. Some of the premium brands offer only one variety, and they recommend feeding more food to puppies and less to elderly dogs than you would feed to normal adult dogs. But since puppies genuinely have different nutritional requirements, it's best to feed your pup a puppy food.

Many brands of "senior" or "lite" foods rely on fillers such as cellulose to reduce the calorie content of the food. This type of food may not be the healthiest option for your overweight or older Boston. In reading labels, you will find that a few brands do not use these fillers; instead, they adjust the balance of the high-quality ingredients to make them appropriate for dogs with special needs.

If you're feeding your dog a homemade diet, check with your veterinarian about the quantity. In general, growing puppies will need a larger quantity of fresh food than adults, with perhaps more protein and fat than adults. Older or overweight dogs will need a smaller quantity of food, with perhaps more vegetables than adult dogs.

Foods to Avoid

The list of foods Boston Terriers can enjoy is quite long, and the list of no-nos is short but important. The four foods you must never feed your Boston Terrier are chocolate, coffee, onions, cooked bones, or alcoholic beverages. Chocolate contains theobromine and caffeine, which can cause vomiting, rapid breathing, seizures, and sometimes death.

Onions contain a substance that can break down red blood cells, leading to a very serious condition called heinz body hemolytic anemia.

Puppies need more calories relative to their size than adult dogs do.

Some things that we humans can eat are toxic to dogs. These include onions, chocolate, coffee, cooked bones, and alcoholic beverages.

Symptoms can include pale gums, blood in the urine, lethargy, depression, weakness, and rapid heartbeat. The symptoms usually appear a few days after the onions have been eaten, when the toxin has destroyed a significant number of the dog's red blood cells. Onions are toxic in any form: raw, cooked or dehydrated.

Never feed your dog cooked bones! Cooking makes the edges too brittle and sharp, and they may puncture the lining of the digestive tract, causing infection and illness. Some breeders do give their dog raw turkey necks or beef hip bones to chew or eat, because these aid digestion and help keep teeth clean.

A small amount of alcohol can cause serious intoxication and even death in pets. It kills off their brains cells, just as it does in humans.

Where and When to Feed

Like people, dogs appreciate eating a meal without interruption, in a quiet spot, and at a regular time. And, just as they do for people, good manners make mealtime more enjoyable for dogs.

Where?

Select a location for your dog that is out of the way but not isolated. Bostons enjoy dining with some company, just not too much. It is only for a few minutes a day, so your Boston should enjoy her meals without the interruption of people walking past or stepping over her while she eats.

Feeding your Boston in the same place every time, such as the kitchen while you're preparing breakfast or having dinner yourself, helps establish good mealtime habits for your dog. You can ask her to sit or lie down before you place the bowl on the floor. This technique helps teach your dog to sit by her place to await her meals, and it reduces her tendency to want to run around barking at you while you're preparing her meals.

When?

Once your dog is about 9 months old, feed her two meals a day. It's easier for dogs to get enough nutrition from their food when they are fed in two meals. These mealtimes should be scheduled, whenever possible, after the human family members have eaten their meals, because the leader in a canine pack always eats first. Try to stick to a regular schedule, more or less (it's okay to sleep in on your day off and delay the weekday crack-of-dawn breakfast).

No Free Lunch

Many dog owners feed one continuous meal—called free feeding—keeping a full bowl of food available at all times. This is a huge no-no.

Although some dogs are able to regulate their own food intake, too many are prone to overeating. Weight is difficult to control in dogs who are free-fed. You will be less likely to notice if your dog loses her appetite, which can be an early sign of illness. When food is available all the time, the food tends to lose its importance and the dog has a harder time identifying the source of the food— her human companions. Finally, many cases of food-bowl guarding, which can lead to dangerous aggression toward other animals or people, begin with a perpetually available bowl of food.

For your dog's twice-daily meals, allow your Boston no more than twenty minutes to eat her meal (most learn to eat in less than five minutes!) before you pick up the bowl.

Bowls

There are many types of food bowls to choose from, including ceramic, crockery, plastic, and stainless steel. While the ceramic dishes look pretty and you can decorate them and even have your dog's name painted on them, stainless steel is a better choice because it is lightweight and easy to clean and disinfect. It will also last a lifetime. Plastic bowls are easy and tempting for the dog to chew. Some dogs have had allergic reactions to plastic bowls, including discoloration of the nose pad and acne around the muzzle.

Crockery bowls tend to be heavy and less convenient to pick up and wash. They also crack and it's too easy for bits of food to become permanently imbedded in the tiny cracks and spoil. Another disadvantage to ceramic or crockery bowls is the possibility of lead in the glaze, which can cause lead poisoning in your Boston.

Stainless steel bowls are a great choice for your dog's food and water.

A Word About Water

Dogs should have fresh drinking water available at all times. This is especially true for Bostons, who are prone to overheat in warm weather and thus need plenty of water to protect against that. A 3-quart stainless steel bowl holds just enough to require filling at least twice a day (three times a day in warmer weather). For most households with one or two Bostons, a 2-quart bowl is probably large enough.

There is some evidence that certain chemicals, such as fluoride and chlorine, found in the tap water of most municipalities may not be healthy for dogs, especially smaller dogs like Bostons. In addition, some older homes have lead pipes, which can add lead to the tap water, and this lead is clearly harmful to dogs. If this concerns you, consider using bottled or filtered water for your Boston.

When you go traveling, take a small water bottle with a built-in filter so that you can provide filtered water for your dog. This is important because changes in water during travel can cause stomach upset and diarrhea. Or you can give your dog bottled water while you're on the road.

Chapter 7

Grooming Your Boston Terrier

When a dog comes permanently dressed in a tuxedo, he doesn't need much more than that to look sharp. Although combat fatigues or a leather jacket may be in style for a Boston these days, all he really needs is some basic sprucing up. A little bit of regular grooming works wonders.

Keeping a Boston Terrier in tip-top shape is all about maintenance. Forget expensive trips to the groomer or long hours brushing and clipping. This is one breed you can easily slick up yourself in no time at all. A Boston is the original ready-to-wear dog who can look good in under an hour.

Bostons aren't big shedders, but there are always a few dog hairs that find their way onto your clothing, furniture, and floors. Bathing and brushing him regularly will help eliminate some flyaway dog hair. One of the joys of having a short-haired dog is not having to do a lot of fussing, but there are a few things that need to be done.

Grooming 101

Grooming a Boston means brushing his teeth and coat, giving him a bath, clipping nails, and cleaning his ears and eyes. There are several good reasons to groom your dog.

First of all, he'll love the pampering and the special attention, and you'll have the opportunity to spend some quality time together. You'll also be able to give your dog's entire body the once over.

A grooming session is a good opportunity to see if he has any lumps or bumps, cuts or rashes, or fleas and ticks, and to examine his mouth for any broken teeth, or swollen or discolored gums. Catch problems right away and you'll be able to obtain treatment for your dog before they get worse.

Besides, keeping your dog clean and fresh just makes him feel good. Who doesn't feel rejuvenated after a shower? Come cuddle time, you'll appreciate snuggling up with your sweet-smelling pal.

When should you begin grooming your Boston? The day after he first comes home. If you've had your dog for a few years and think it's too late to begin a new habit, guess again. It's never too late. It may take a little longer to train him to stand still while you brush him and trim his nails, but patience, perseverance, and lots of treats will go a long way.

Set aside a few moments every day to run your hands all over your dog's body and give him a small food treat. That way he'll look forward to you touching him. Once he becomes accustomed to being handled, you can progress to brushing his body and his teeth, clipping his nails, giving him a bath, and cleaning his ears and eyes. Choose one day a week when you're not rushed and can take the time you need.

Grooming Tools

Here's what you'll need:

- Soft bristle brush and rubber brush
- Flea comb
- Nonskid mat for sink or bathtub
- Spray nozzle attachment for sink or tub
- Cotton balls and gauze pads
- Baby or dog shampoo
- Medicated shampoo (for problem skin)
- Coat conditioner (optional)
- Pet hair dryer or cotton bath towels
- Ear-cleaning solution
- Nail clipper or cordless, battery-operated pet nail grinder
- Styptic powder or pencil (a coagulating agent)
- Canine toothbrush and canine toothpaste

A luxury item that comes in handy is a grooming table with a nonskid surface and a grooming noose. Putting your dog up on the table makes it much easier to brush him and clip his toenails without having to bend over. The noose holds his head in place and prevents him from moving around too much. Even with the noose on, and whenever your dog is standing on any elevated surface,

A grooming table is a welcome luxury, so you don't have to bend over your Boston.

keep one hand on your dog at all times! It doesn't take much for your Boston to go too close to the edge, fall off, and injure himself.

If a grooming table and noose aren't in your budget, you can also use an outdoor picnic table, the kitchen counter, or the bathroom counter, and ask someone to help hold your dog still for you. Use a rubber-backed plastic tablecloth or a bathmat on top of these surfaces to keep your dog's feet from sliding.

Gather together everything you need before you put your dog in the tub or up on the table. Nothing's worse that having a wet dog and realizing you forgot something you need.

The Body Brush-Off

It just takes a few minutes to brush a Boston Terrier, so it's easy to do it every day. If that isn't convenient, once a week will do, too. Dog hair grows in cycles, which take 125 to 135 days to complete. Normally hair grows, stops growing, dries out, and sheds. Bostons tend to keep more of their coats during the cold winter months, but come summer, they'll shed some of the extra hair.

There are several good reasons to brush your dog. It distributes natural oils, removes dead hair, promotes new hair growth, and gives your dog's coat a shiny, velvety look. A Boston should look sleek and glossy and his coat should naturally radiate good health.

Brush your Boston all over at least once a week.

If his coat is dull and brittle or dry and flaky, this could be a sign of allergies, parasites, an inferior diet, or not enough grooming. A clean, healthy Boston should not have an odor, either.

Begin brushing at his head and continue in one long stroke toward the tail before moving down the legs and along the sides. Brush gently but firmly in the direction the hair grows. Follow up the brushing action with a flea comb—a metal one is best—to pick up any fleas or ticks. There's more about these pests later on in this chapter.

Be on the lookout for any open wounds your dog has, as well as bumps, swollen areas, or splinters. Contact your veterinarian if there's a spot that concerns you.

When the last hair is in place, wipe your dog down with a damp towel or give his coat a spritz from a spray bottle filled with water with two or three tablespoons of Listerine added in. This gives his coat a healthy shine.

Bathing Your Boston

If you're brushing him regularly, you'll eliminate some of the dirt and grime, but brushing alone won't get rid of the natural oil build-up that's responsible for that special doggy aroma. Here's where dog shampoo and water come in handy.

Where your dog spends most of his time and how dirty he gets determines how often you will bathe him. If he's indoors a lot, a bath once a month is probably sufficient. Fortunately, Bostons aren't the down-and-dirty type, but if you happen to have a fellow who enjoys a good romp in the mud, he'll definitely need a bath sooner than you might have planned.

You can bathe your Boston in your kitchen sink or in the bath tub, but first put a small rubber bathmat on the bottom to prevent your dog from sliding. A spray hose attachment makes the job a lot easier, although a plastic pitcher for wetting and rinsing works well, too.

Tub Training

The first few times you bathe your dog may be wet and wild, especially if he keeps trying to escape. Be patient. You can teach him to like the water by giving him a treat when you first put him into the tub and again when you take him out. Spend a few days putting him into the tub for just a few moments without the water running and give him a treat. When he's comfortable with the experience, work up to having the water running and be sure to praise him and give him a treat. This way he'll begin to associate bathing with positive experiences.

Assemble everything you need before you start bathing. This way you won't have to leave your dog alone in the tub (and ready to jump out) while you run to get something. If it's cold out, check to be sure there isn't a draft coming from a vent or an open window. Your Boston won't like the spa experience if he's cold.

You can bathe your dog outdoors only if the weather is warm.

To keep water from getting into his ears, gently place a cotton ball in each ear. Don't press it in too far and don't forget to take it out when you're done bathing him.

Can you bathe your dog outdoors with the garden hose? Maybe, if the weather is very warm and the water in the faucet isn't cold. Attach a sprayer nozzle so you can regulate the water pressure. A straight, forceful stream will sting your dog.

The Spa Experience

When you're ready to begin bathing indoors, put your dog in the tub but don't fill it with water. Test the temperature of the water on the inside of your wrist to make sure it's not too hot or too cold. Next, wet him thoroughly and apply a small amount of either mild baby shampoo or doggy shampoo on his back, chest, neck, and hindquarters. For dogs with skin problems, your veterinarian can recommend a medicated shampoo.

Using the rubber brush, massage the shampoo gently into his coat. With your fingertips, rub a small amount of shampoo on your dog's head. You can also use a washcloth to soap up your Boston's head. Don't get any soap in his eyes! If you do, rinse it out with clean water right away.

When you're done shampooing, thoroughly rinse off all of the soap. Leftover soap residue will produce dull, flaky skin and make your dog itch. Apply coat conditioner, if you're using it, after you're done rinsing. Place a towel over your dog to prevent him from shaking water all over the room!

Dry your dog off with thick, all-cotton towels or use a canine hair dryer on a low temperature if you're in a hurry. If it's a warm day, your dog can probably air dry once you've toweled him off.

Clean Teeth

If you have a puppy, he will lose his baby teeth when he's 3 to 6 months old. When his adult teeth come in, they're shiny white. To keep them looking like that, they must be brushed once a day. Just before brushing, check his mouth to make sure it is healthy. Healthy gums should be pink, and never red or puffy. Your dog's teeth should never be broken or dirty because they harbor bacteria that can affect the heart and kidneys.

According to the American Veterinary Dental Society (AVDS), 80 percent of dogs develop gum disease by 3 years of age. With regular veterinary dental checkups and daily brushing at home, your dog can avoid dental disease.

It's very important to brush your Boston Terrier's teeth once a day. The breed is prone to having large teeth that are crowded too closely together in the mouth, which creates spaces for bits of food to get trapped and decay.

Use a doggy toothbrush and doggy toothpaste. This brush fits a dog's mouth and the toothpaste is specially formulated for dogs. It doesn't need rinsing because it dissolves in the mouth and dogs usually love the flavor. Don't use toothpaste made for people; it will give your dog an upset stomach.

Begin introducing the toothbrush and paste the day after your puppy or adult dog comes home. Put some toothpaste on your finger and rub it over one of your dog's teeth. Your Boston will begin licking the toothpaste. That's okay. Repeat this for a few more days. When your dog seems comfortable with the process, put toothpaste on the brush and just touch the brush to the teeth. A few days later, gradually move to the rear molars or around the front of the teeth. It won't take long for your dog to look forward to his daily dental hygiene appointment.

Nail Trimming

If you hear clicking every time your dog walks across the floor, his nails are much too long! They should never curl over the pads of the feet. When nails have grown out too much, they can lead to foot problems or break or tear while the dog is running or playing.

Walking on concrete doesn't automatically keep nails short. Like people, some dogs just have nails that grow faster and longer than others do. All dogs need to have their nails trimmed once a week, or once every two weeks if they grow more slowly.

To clip your dog's nails, put him up on a table. Ask someone to assist, if possible. The first few times you won't actually be trimming all of the nails. Just show your dog the clippers (or the electric nail grinder) and get him to let you handle his feet—and be patient, because this may take some time.

When your dog seems okay with letting you touch his feet, take one paw, hold it gently, and choose one nail to hold between your thumb and your finger. Trim off the tip of the nail where there is a slight hook.

Get your dog accustomed to having his feet handled when he is a puppy and he won't fuss about having his nails trimmed.

New Products in the Fight Against Fleas

At one time, battling fleas meant exposing your dog and yourself to toxic dips, sprays, powders, and collars. But today there are flea preventives that work very well and are safe for your dog, you, and the environment. The two most common types are insect growth regulators (IGRs), which stop the immature flea from developing or maturing, and adult flea killers. To deal with an active infestation, experts usually recommend a product that has both.

These next-generation flea fighters generally come in one of two forms:

- **Topical treatments or spot-ons.** These products are applied to the skin, usually between the shoulder blades. The product is absorbed through the skin into the dog's system. Among the most widely available spot-ons are Advantage (kills adult fleas and larvae), Revolution (kills adult fleas), Frontline Plus (kills adult fleas and larvae, plus an IGR), K-9 Advantix (kills adult fleas and larvae), and BioSpot (kills adult fleas and larvae, plus an IGR).
- **Systemic products.** This is a pill your dog swallows that transmits a chemical throughout the dog's bloodstream. When a flea bites the dog, it picks up this chemical, which then prevents the flea's eggs from developing. Among the most widely available systemic products are Program (kills larvae only, plus an IGR) and Capstar (kills adult fleas).

Make sure you read all the labels and apply the products exactly as recommended, and that you check to make sure they are safe for puppies.

Avoid hitting the quick, which is the blood vessel you can see inside the nail. If you accidentally clip it, quickly dip the toe into styptic powder. When you've finished clipping a nail, give your dog a small food treat to reward him for letting you take care of him.

When your dog realizes that having his nails trimmed isn't so bad after all, you can add another nail or two each time until you can trim all of them in one session. Always offer a food treat after you clip each nail and your dog will look forward to the special bonding time.

Cleaning Ears

The Boston Terrier has naturally erect ears. A healthy ear is clean and odor-free, without any discharge.

A good grooming routine includes ear cleaning. Once a week, check your dog's ears to make sure that they don't have a black or brown waxy discharge or a strong odor. If so, schedule a visit with your veterinarian. Your veterinarian can recommend a liquid ear cleaner and demonstrate how to clean out the discharge and keep the ears clean all the time.

When you clean your dog's ears, you'll need a few long strips of cotton or cotton balls, and the medicated cleaner. Squeeze a small amount of the cleaner into

Bostons have open ears and big eyes, and both must be cleaned regularly.

Making Your Environment Flea Free

If there are fleas on your dog, there are fleas in your home, yard, and car, even if you can't see them. Take these steps to combat them.

In your home:

- Wash whatever is washable (the dog bed, sheets, blankets, pillow covers, slipcovers, curtains, etc.).
- Vacuum everything else in your home—furniture, floors, rugs, everything. Pay special attention to the folds and crevices in upholstery, cracks between floorboards, and the spaces between the floor and the baseboards. Flea larvae are sensitive to sunlight, so inside the house they prefer deep carpet, bedding, and cracks and crevices.
- When you're done, throw the vacuum cleaner bag away—in an outside garbage can.
- Use a nontoxic flea-killing powder, such as Flea Busters or Zodiac FleaTrol, to treat your carpets (but remember, it does not control fleas elsewhere in the house). The powder stays deep in the carpet and kills fleas (using a form of boric acid) for up to a year.
- If you have a particularly serious flea problem, consider using a fogger or long-lasting spray to kill any adult and larval fleas, or having a professional exterminator treat your home.

your dog's ear and gently massage the ear to work the solution around. Quickly insert the cotton ball before your dog has a chance to shake his head and scatter the cleaner. Wipe around the inside of the ear with the cotton. Repeat a few times with clean cotton on the same ear until there's no discharge on the cotton. Clean the other ear the same way.

Eye Care

Occasionally your Boston's eyes may have a clear, slight discharge. Wipe it away with a gauze pad and some warm water. Begin at the inside corner of the eye and wipe toward the outside corner.

If there is any swelling in the eye or your dog has difficulty opening his eye, contact your veterinarian or a veterinary ophthalmologist. Your dog may have an infection or an eye problem.

In your car:

- Take out the floor mats and hose them down with a strong stream of water, then hang them up to dry in the sun.
- Wash any towels, blankets, or other bedding you regularly keep in the car.
- Thoroughly vacuum the entire interior of your car, paying special attention to the seams between the bottom and back of the seats.
- When you're done, throw the vacuum cleaner bag away—in an outside garbage can.

In your yard:

- Flea larvae prefer shaded areas that have plenty of organic material and moisture, so rake the yard thoroughly and bag all the debris in tightly sealed bags.
- Spray your yard with an insecticide that has residual activity for at least thirty days. Insecticides that use a form of boric acid are non-toxic. Some newer products contain an insect growth regulator (such as fenoxycarb) and need to be applied only once or twice a year.
- For an especially difficult flea problem, consider having an exterminator treat your yard.
- Keep your yard free of piles of leaves, weeds, and other organic debris. Be especially careful in shady, moist areas, such as under bushes.

Fleas and Ticks, Oh My

Got dog? If so, there's always the possibility that he may have fleas or ticks some time during his life. But he doesn't have to keep them. Your grooming sessions are a great way to examine your dog up close and personal to see if he has any of these external varmints.

The sooner you find the little parasites, the quicker you can get rid of them before they have a chance to wreak havoc on your dog's health.

Fleas

Fleas aren't so easy to see on a Boston because these black parasites are the same color as your dog's coat and they blend right in. Brush or use a flea comb on your Boston in a well-lit room or outdoors and you'll be able to spot fleas a little more easily. A fine-toothed flea comb is designed to pick up fleas and ticks. They

How to Get Rid of a Tick

Although Frontline, K-9 Advantix, and BioSpot, the new gener-
ation of flea fighters, are partially effective in killing ticks once
they are on your dog, they are not 100 percent effective and will
not keep ticks from biting your dog in the first place. During tick
season (which, depending on where you live, can be spring,
summer, and/or fall), examine your dog every day for ticks. Pay
particular attention to your dog's neck, behind the ears, the
armpits, and the groin.

When you find a tick, use a pair of tweezers to grasp the tick
as close as possible to the dog's skin and pull it out using firm,
steady pressure. Check to make sure you get the whole tick
(mouth parts left in your dog's skin can cause an infection), then
dab the wound with a little hydrogen peroxide and some
antibiotic ointment. Watch for signs of inflammation.

Ticks carry very serious diseases that are transmittable to
humans, so dispose of the tick safely. *Never* crush it between
your fingers. Don't flush it down the toilet either, because the
tick will survive the trip and infect another animal. Instead, use
the tweezers to place the tick in a tight-sealing jar or plastic
dish with a little alcohol, put on the lid, and dispose of the con-
tainer in an outdoor garbage can. Wash the tweezers thoroughly with hot water and alcohol.

like to hang around your dog's tail area, hips, and underneath his body, although
it's not unusual for them to appear on the chest and head, too. If you pick one
up on your dog, dip it in a bowl of hot water you have handy, so it doesn't live
to bite another day.

Fleas leave flea dirt, which looks like tiny bits of pepper, but with your
Boston's black or brindle coat you may not be able to see it. If you see flea dirt in
the flea comb after combing your dog, it means that he does have fleas and they
are burrowing deep into your dog's coat.

If you happen to discover a flea on your dog and try to pick it off, good luck!
Fleas move fast. They'll be crawling along one area of the skin one minute, then

leaping and diving into your dog's coat the next.

There's no such thing as just one flea, either. Where there's one, there's usually dozens more you can't see. From egg to adult, the average life span of a flea is two weeks to eight months. During that time the female lays 15 to 20 eggs per day and up to 600 during her lifetime.

Why try to wipe out these pests? Fleas irritate and bite your dog, making him itch, scratch, and bite himself. They can also cause an allergic reaction producing red or swollen blotches, and they are capable of transmitting tapeworm and a variety of illnesses.

There are many flea sprays, dips, shampoos, collars, and flea bombs available for this purpose, but it's much easier to prevent them from

Use a fine-toothed comb to regularly check your dog for fleas and ticks.

showing up to begin with. Your veterinarian has several different kinds of flea and tick prevention and management programs available, and there are other products that you can purchase at pet supply stores or through mail-order catalogs without a prescription (see the box on page 72).

Ticks

Your grooming session should also include thoroughly checking your dog for the presence of any ticks. Because of their dark brown or black color and variety of sizes, they're not easy to find. Immature ticks are about the size of a poppy seed; adult ticks are about the size of a sesame seed.

Use a flea comb to comb your Boston and you may find a tick clinging to your dog's coat. Ticks like to hang out on your dog's head or neck, although your dog's chest, armpits, and groin are other favorite locales. Look between his toes and inside his ears, too. Yuck!

If you do find one, don't panic! Remove it immediately but don't touch a tick with your fingers because it can infect you. Ticks carry Lyme disease and other ailments, such as Rocky Mountain spotted fever, which are dangerous to both dogs and people. Pull out the tick as described in the box on page 76.

Chapter 8

Keeping Your Boston Terrier Healthy

L ike their sturdy New England ancestors, Boston Terriers are hardy dogs. Sure, there's always the chance that your dog will accidentally injure herself or develop a hereditary disease, but with good care, the breed is pretty healthy overall.

Your job is to make sure your dog stays in tip-top shape. This means providing quality veterinary and preventive care, feeding her a nutritious diet, and keeping her at a healthy weight. With an average life span of ten to thirteen years, your Boston can have a long and active life, but to remain healthy she'll need a complete series of vaccinations, spaying or neutering, good dental care, and proper exercise.

Finding a Veterinarian

If you don't already have a veterinarian, you'll need to choose one before your new Boston comes home. Having a reputable, knowledgeable veterinarian you feel comfortable with and whom you can trust is one of the best things you can do to safeguard your dog's health. This professional has your Boston's best interests at heart and treats your dog with respect. This vet takes care of any medical problems to the best of their ability and doesn't hesitate to refer you to a specialist, if necessary.

To locate a veterinarian, contact the American Animal Hospital Association (see the appendix). You can also ask dog owners in your neighborhood for the names of vets they recommend. If your dog's breeder lives nearby, she can give you the name of her veterinarian, or if she's far away she should be able to network with other Boston breeders and owners in your area to find a good veterinarian for you.

When it's time to narrow your search, call the vet's office and ask if you can schedule an appointment to tour the office and meet with the veterinarian for a few minutes, with or without your dog. You should expect to pay for this time. This gives you a chance to see how clean the facilities are and to chat with the vet before there's a problem with your dog. If your dog ever needs to spend the day in the hospital, you'll want to see what it looks like.

Some veterinary clinics hold an open house once or twice a year, usually on a weekend, and invite people to have a look behind the scenes. You'll have a chance to see amazing medical equipment, the operating room, and the laboratory. The best part is being able to chat with the veterinarian and the staff informally and to learn more about the office philosophy on treating patients.

What to Ask the Vet

During your interviews with the veterinarian, ask what her credentials are—what veterinary school she graduated from and if she specialized in a particular area of medicine. You can also ask how many other Bostons she has treated in her career and what problems they have had. Although it's nice to have a vet who sees a lot of Boston Terriers in her practice, don't expect it. A reputable veterinarian knows about Boston problems and keeps up with the latest health developments.

Ask how many other veterinarians are on staff and if you can request the same doctor at each visit. More than one vet in the office ensures that you will be able to see a doctor when you need one. But for routine care, it's best to stick to one doctor who knows you and your dog.

Find out if the office is open after hours for emergencies, or if the vet refers patients to an emergency animal clinic after regular hours. It's best to know this information before you ever need it.

Learn something about the office staff and technicians, too, and what qualifications are required to work there. These people will be assisting the veterinarian and handling your dog, so it's important to have people who are competent and personable.

Find a good veterinarian before you bring your dog home. An emergency is not the time to first start looking for a vet.

Why Spay and Neuter?

Breeding dogs is a serious undertaking that should only be part of a well-planned breeding program. Why? Because dogs pass on their physical and behavioral problems to their offspring. Even healthy, well-behaved dogs can pass on problems in their genes.

Is your dog so sweet that you'd like to have a litter of puppies just like her? If you breed her to another dog, the pups will not have the same genetic heritage she has. Breeding her *parents* again will increase the odds of a similar pup, but even then, the puppies in the second litter could inherit different genes. In fact, *there is no way to breed a dog to be just like another dog.*

Meanwhile, thousands and thousands of dogs are killed in animal shelters every year simply because they have no homes. Casual breeding is a big contributor to this problem.

If you don't plan to breed your dog, is it still a good idea to spay her or neuter him? Yes!

When you spay your female:

- You avoid her heat cycles, during which she discharges blood and scent.
- It greatly reduces the risk of mammary cancer and eliminates the risk of pyometra (an often fatal infection of the uterus) and uterine cancer.
- It prevents unwanted pregnancies.
- It reduces dominance behaviors and aggression.

When you neuter your male:

- It curbs the desire to roam and to fight with other males.
- It greatly reduces the risk of prostate cancer and eliminates the risk of testicular cancer.
- It helps reduce leg lifting and mounting behavior.
- It reduces dominance behaviors and aggression.

Overall, look for a veterinary office with employees who are knowledgeable, friendly, helpful, and genuinely like dogs. You'll want a home-away-from-home type of atmosphere where the staff can assure you that your dog is being well taken care of.

The veterinarian you ultimately select should explain any medical information in terms you can easily understand, be patient with your questions, and like your dog. You should never feel rushed and always feel comfortable talking with the veterinarian. If you don't like the way the veterinarian speaks with you, it doesn't matter what her credentials are or who recommended her, because she's not the veterinarian for you.

Holistic Options

The type of treatment a veterinarian offers may be important to you and your dog. Many veterinarians use conventional medicine to treat their patients; others use holistic medicine in their practices. Holistic is a combination of alternative treatments such as acupuncture, chiropractic care, and botanical and homeopathic remedies.

According to the American Holistic Veterinary Association (AHVA), holistic techniques are gentle, minimally invasive, and incorporate patient well-being and stress reduction. Some veterinarians combine conventional and alternative methods.

If holistic medicine is important to you, you can find a veterinarian who shares your view.

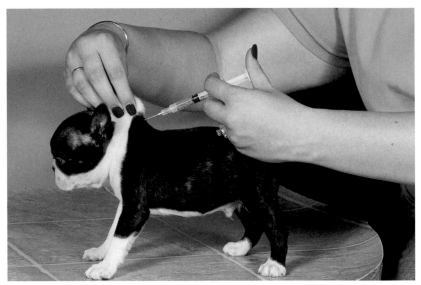

Vaccinations will be part of your dog's preventive care regimen. What shots a dog needs, and when, depends on the dog.

When qualified veterinarians use holistic and conventional methods, they can offer your Boston a full range of treatment possibilities. There are times when some dog owners are willing to try anything that will help their dogs live a longer life.

To find holistic veterinarians, contact the AHVA (see the appendix).

The First Visit

Schedule an appointment for your new Boston to see the veterinarian within two or three days of bringing her home. Your dog may look healthy to you, but the veterinarian may be able to spot a problem.

During this initial visit, the vet will listen to your dog's heart and lungs, take her temperature, measure her weight, and examine her coat, skin, eyes, ears, feet, and mouth. Bring along a fresh stool specimen that will reveal whether your dog has any internal parasites.

The veterinarian will want to know what kind of food your dog is eating, how much and how often you are feeding her, and if you've noticed she has any problems.

Feel free to discuss an overall health care plan for your Boston, including flea, tick, and heartworm preventives, when to spay her (or neuter him), when she needs to return to the office for vaccines, and, if you have a puppy, when to change her diet from a puppy recipe to an adult one.

Preventive Care

Your veterinarian will want to monitor your dog's health by seeing her for a routine checkup once a year. Sometimes it may not seem like your Boston needs to see the doctor, but a lot can happen in a dog's life in twelve months. The annual checkup monitors your dog's overall health and your veterinarian can detect any problems with her skin, eyes, teeth, heart, kidneys, or liver. As your Boston ages, there's a chance that she may develop cancer or skin or eye problems, and your veterinarian may be able to spot these early on. It may also be time for your dog to receive a vaccination or two (see the box on page 84).

Maintaining a Healthy Weight

Keeping your dog at the proper weight improves her chances of living a long and healthy life. Boston Terriers love food (who doesn't?), and yours will gladly consume all the goodies you give her. If you're not careful, she'll look like a black and white sausage in no time at all.

Carrying too much weight adds pressure to your dog's heart and legs and hampers her ability to move around comfortably and breathe properly. When your dog weighs what she's supposed to, you should be able to feel but not see her ribs. Looking down at her from over the top, her body should have a definite shape to it with an indentation where her ribs end and her loin begins.

Getting Enough Exercise

Boston Terriers need plenty of exercise to keep them in good health. Getting out and burning off some energy (and calories) will help stimulate your dog's respiratory and circulatory systems and strengthen her bones and muscular development. As with people, exercise enriches a dog's mind and banishes boredom and loneliness—two reasons why dogs bark too much or chew up your couch cushions.

Start slowly! If your Boston has been a couch potato, begin an

A puppy can have shorter and more frequent exercise sessions, while an adult can do more, but less often.

Vaccines

What vaccines dogs need and how often they need them has been a subject of controversy for several years. Researchers, health care professionals, vaccine manufacturers, and dog owners do not always agree on which vaccines each dog needs or how often booster shots must be given.

In 2006, the American Animal Hospital Association issued a set of vaccination guidelines and recommendations intended to help dog owners and veterinarians sort through much of the controversy and conflicting information. The guidelines designate four vaccines as core, or essential for every dog, because of the serious nature of the diseases and their widespread distribution. These are canine distemper virus (using a modified live virus or recombinant modified live virus vaccine), canine parvovirus (using a modified live virus vaccine), canine adenovirus-2 (using a modified live virus vaccine), and rabies (using a killed virus). The general recommendations for their administration (except rabies, for which you must follow local laws) are:

- Vaccinate puppies at 6–8 weeks, 9–11 weeks, and 12–14 weeks.
- Give an initial "adult" vaccination when the dog is older than 16 weeks; two doses, three to four weeks apart, are

exercise program gradually. Don't take her out the first time and expect her to jog beside you for five miles.

Although puppies seem to have a boundless supply of energy, too much exercise or excessive game playing can actually do more harm than good. Puppy bones and muscles are still developing and can easily be injured. Limit the jumping, especially, for a young puppy with growing bones.

How do you know if the amount of exercise you give your Boston is too much or not enough? A puppy can have shorter, more frequent exercise sessions throughout the day, while an adult Boston can probably build up to walking a advised, but one dose is considered protective and acceptable.

- Give a booster shot when the dog is 1 year old.
- Give a subsequent booster shot every three years, unless there are risk factors that make it necessary to vaccinate more or less often.

Noncore vaccines should only be considered for those dogs who risk exposure to a particular disease because of geographic area, lifestyle, frequency of travel, or other issues. They include vaccines against distemper-measles virus, canine parainfluenza virus, leptospirosis, Bordetella bronchiseptica, and Borrelia burgdorferi (Lyme disease).

Vaccines that are not generally recommended because the disease poses little risk to dogs or is easily treatable, or the vaccine has not been proven to be effective, are those against Giardia, canine coronavirus, and canine adenovirus-1.

Often, combination injections are given to puppies, with one shot containing several core and noncore vaccines. Your veterinarian may be reluctant to use separate shots that do not include the noncore vaccines, because they must be specially ordered. If you are concerned about these noncore vaccines, talk to your vet.

mile or two. Don't forget that running after a ball, either indoors or outside in a fenced area, counts as exercise!

Watching the Weather

It's a fact: Black dogs retain more heat than light-colored dogs do. Add the Boston's short, thin coat and her short, flat muzzle, and she's at a higher risk for heatstroke than breeds with thicker coats and longer muzzles. Longer muzzles allow more air to circulate through the dog's nose and mouth and act as a cooling device.

During hot weather, limit your outings to early morning or early evening when the weather is cooler. If your dog is staying outside for any length of time, she'll need plenty of fresh water and a shady spot where she can cool off.

Never leave your dog in a parked car, even with all the windows open a little. The temperature inside the car can heat up to 102 degrees Fahrenheit in ten minutes and continues to rise after that. If a dog's temperature rises to 107 degrees (normal body temperature is 101.5 to 102.2 degrees), she may suffer irreparable brain damage or even death.

Internal Parasites

Internal parasites include worms and protozoa. With some, the parasites are evident in the dog's stool. With others, you might not be aware that your dog has them until you notice that she has lost a lot of weight despite a very healthy appetite, or she has an unusually rounded abdomen. Other symptoms include a lackluster coat, dull eyes, weakness, coughing, vomiting, and diarrhea.

If you suspect that your dog has parasites, take a fresh stool sample to your veterinarian for analysis.

Parasites lurk everywhere outdoors, and all dogs are susceptible.

Worms, Yuck!

The most common internal parasites are roundworms, whipworms, tapeworms, and hookworms. These worms live in the canine digestive tract, where some feed on nutrients being absorbed into the intestinal walls and others feed on the dog's blood, through the intestinal wall.

Except for tapeworms, these parasites are usually spread through feces. When an infected dog defecates on the ground, the feces contain the parasite eggs. Dogs become infected by eating the feces containing the eggs, stepping in it and licking their paws, or walking on soil that has been contaminated by infected feces and licking their paws.

Once your veterinarian makes a diagnosis, she can prescribe medication to kill and eliminate the worms. Some of the monthly heartworm preventives also help prevent infection from roundworms, hookworms, and whipworms. Controlling fleas in your dog's environment will help prevent tapeworms.

Giardia

Giardia is a single-cell parasite that is transmitted through contaminated drinking water. If your dog's stool is light-colored, foul-smelling, and mucuousy or bloody, giardia could be the culprit.

To diagnose it, your veterinarian will ask you to bring in a stool sample and can prescribe a course of treatment to ease the discomfort.

Coccidia

There's a strong likelihood that puppies who live in crowded conditions, such as pet shops, kennels, puppy mills, and animal shelters, may contract coccidia, an intestinal parasite. It spreads through contaminated food or water and causes bloating, bloody stool, straining during elimination, vomiting, and weight loss.

Coccidia can be prevented by promptly cleaning up feces and cleaning the kennel area with an antiseptic solution. It's a good idea to pick up your dog's stools every day, to keep her and your family healthy.

Heartworm

Heartworm is a deadly parasite that develops in the canine bloodstream and is carried by mosquitoes from one dog to another as a microscopic larva. In its mature form, it is a large worm that burrows into the dog's heart, obstructing the blood flow and causing coughing and shortness of breath.

The advanced condition is very serious and may be life-threatening. Veterinarians treat heartworm by using extremely toxic substances to kill the worms. The treatment itself can make a dog who is already sick much worse.

Prevention is therefore key in dealing with heartworm. The best way to protect your dog from heartworm disease is to regularly give your dog the oral preventive prescribed by your veterinarian.

Health Problems Seen in Bostons

There are health problems that are inherited (genetic) or congenital (present at birth but not necessarily genetic). No breed is free from health problems, and

Bostons have their share, but not as many as other breeds. However, with proper care, some problems can be avoided.

Responsible breeders are aware of the breed's health issues and are doing what they can to prevent them. To promote good health and sound breeding, the Boston Terrier Club of America formed the BTCA Health Committee in 1999. The committee established a voluntary health certification program for BTCA members whose dogs complete a physical examination for genetic disease, and pass the Orthopedic Foundation for Animals (OFA) test for strong patellas, the Canine Eye Registration Certification (CERF) eye tests, and the Brainstem Auditory Evoked Response (BAER) hearing tests.

Dogs who are affected with genetic health problems should not be bred and are usually removed from breeding programs. However, even healthy parents can produce puppies with genetic or environmentally induced congenital defects.

When purchasing a Boston Terrier from a reputable breeder, ask if the puppy or the dog's parents have passed health clearances for specific breed problems and have a BTCA Health Certificate.

Brachycephalic Syndrome

The Boston's flat face and short muzzle give her a unique appearance. Unfortunately, these compressed facial features make breathing more difficult, causing many Bostons to have noisy mouth breathing, foamy nostrils, coughing, and regurgitation of foamy saliva.

That adorable short muzzle can cause breathing problems.

Extremely narrow nostrils (stenotic nares) or an elongated soft palate, which hangs down in the throat and obstructs the dog's airway, are responsible for this noisy breathing. Both problems can be corrected surgically.

When your Boston goes outdoors on a warm day, take special care to keep her cool. Overheating can easily lead to heat exhaustion.

Cancer

All types of cancers affect nearly every breed, although many short-nosed breeds are susceptible to a certain type of brain tumor, known as a glioma. This tumor can be slow-growing and benign or highly aggressive and malignant.

A veterinary neurologist can perform diagnostic tests, including a CT (sometimes called CAT) scan, MRI, or surgical biopsy. Today, the treatment options for dogs are very similar to those used for people: surgery, radiation, and chemotherapy. Depending upon the location and size of the cancer, treatment can be very expensive and emotionally draining for both dog and owner.

Deafness

Boston Terriers can be born deaf in one ear or in both ears. This kind of hereditary deafness occurs because the blood vessels in the inner ear degenerate. When that happens, the nerve cells in the ear die and there is deafness. The condition is irreversible. According to the BTCA health survey, about 3.8 percent of Bostons are born deaf.

If a dog is deaf in one ear, there is some hearing and she can live a normal life and be an excellent pet. A totally deaf dog will have unique training challenges. While some deaf dogs may develop aggressive or anxious tendencies, others have normal behavior.

Most breeders can usually detect deaf puppies as young as 4 weeks of age, but a veterinarian with BAER (brainstem auditory evoked response) testing equipment can test puppies at 5 or 6 weeks of age. BAER hearing testing is a painless laboratory procedure that measures the brain's response to certain sounds. The results can be printed. Puppies do not need to be sedated during testing.

Conscientious breeders have all their litters BAER hearing tested. If you are buying a Boston Terrier, ask the breeder for a copy of the BAER hearing test so you know the dog's hearing status.

Eye Problems

Big, beautiful, googly but protruding eyes may be cute, but they are also vulnerable to eye injuries. Protect your dog from sun exposure with a doggy visor and don't allow her to stick her head out of the car window because strong gusts of wind and dust particles can scratch her corneas. Keep rose bushes, cacti, and any thorny plants out of bounds in your yard, and avoid having anything sharp at your dog's eye level.

Eye scratches can be diagnosed and treated by your regular vet, and they usually resolve in a couple of days. However, you must follow your vet's instructions carefully and return to the vet if the eye gets worse or doesn't improve within twenty-four to forty-eight hours. Without treatment, corneal scratches can ulcerate and the dog may lose her eye.

Some Bostons have problems with tear stains or weepy eyes. Allergies, clogged, or blocked tear ducts, or an improper diet may cause this condition. Work with your vet to determine and treat the cause. If left untreated, the condition may cause an infection that could damage the eye.

Juvenile Cataracts

A cataract is any opacity in the lens of the eye. Inherited types of cataracts—mostly juvenile but also senior—are the most prevalent health problem in the breed. According to the 2000 BTCA Health Survey of 1,903 dogs, about 2.4 percent of Boston Terriers had juvenile cataracts.

In very young dogs, cataracts cause early blindness. There is no medical treatment available to reverse cataracts or to prevent or shrink them. A veterinary ophthalmologist can perform surgery on some types of cataracts to remove the lens, but it gives the dog only limited vision and is very expensive.

Those big, protruding eyes are vulnerable to injuries.

Corneal Ulcers

There are more than twenty different eye diseases that affect Bostons, but corneal ulcers are the second largest eye problem in the breed. According to the BTCA Health survey, one Boston in ten will experience a corneal ulcer sometime during her life.

A corneal ulcer is caused by an abrasion from just about anything—a bee sting, a scratch from a thorn or a claw, or a rub from a paw. Once the smooth surface of the cornea is scratched, it quickly becomes infected, making the eye painful and irritating. When a dog has a corneal ulcer, she will squint and rub her eye and will produce a lot of tears.

Hemivertebrae

Hemivertebrae is a malformation of one of the bones of the spine (the vertebrae), in which a bone is smaller than normal and is oddly shaped. Nearly every Boston has at least one hemivertebra in her tail; this is what causes the screw tail.

Hemivertebrae can also occur in other parts of the spine. Usually there are no outward signs. In unusual cases, the bone is so small and misshapen that there isn't enough space for the spinal cord to pass through, resulting in pinched nerves, pain, and paralysis.

Ingrown Tails

Corkscrew or ingrown tails can be a serious problem. The tail grows backward and down into the rectum, which creates a deep crevice where the tail would normally be attached. The area is painful and requires veterinary attention and regular cleaning so it does not become infected. Often, the tail must be amputated.

Patella Luxation

The most common genetic problem in Boston Terriers is patella luxation, also known as dislocated kneecaps. It happens when the patella (kneecap) slips in and out of the groove at the lower end of the femur (the large bone in the thigh). This health problem can be painful and crippling, and causes limping that ranges from slight to severe.

Your veterinarian or a veterinary orthopedist can X-ray the dog's kneecaps and diagnose the problem according to how severe the defect is. On a scale of 1 to 4, with 1 being minor and 4 being most severe, the vet can grade the degree of luxation in the kneecaps. This information can be registered with the Orthopedic Foundation of America (OFA), although registration is optional.

Surgery can correct abnormalities that are 3s or 4s by anchoring the kneecap to prevent it from slipping out of place. Surgery is not recommended for 1s or 2s because the dog will probably not feel any pain anyway, unless she is jumping.

Skin Problems

All dogs can be affected by skin problems, but according to the BTCA health survey, almost one-fifth of Bostons are affected by skin allergies. Other causes of itchy skin are parasites (see chapter 7), bacterial infections, and fungal infections.

A veterinarian can ascertain the soundness of your dog's knees and hips.

Atopic Dermatitis

Bostons with atopic dermatitis are hypersensitive to environmental allergens, such as grass and weed pollens, house-dust mites, molds, and other allergens. These cause itchy skin, particularly around the feet, ears, and face.

The problem can begin when the dog is 6 months to 3 years of age. For relief, a veterinarian or veterinary dermatologist may prescribe fatty-acid supplements, bathing with hypoallergenic shampoos, and avoiding known allergens.

Skin Allergies

Parasites, pollens, certain foods, drugs, chemicals, and dust can trigger an allergic response in a hypersensitive dog. A veterinary dermatologist can perform skin tests to determine the allergens.

Some dogs are highly allergic to flea bites and will scratch nonstop to alleviate the irritation. To give some relief to your dog, treat the dog and the environment to eliminate fleas (see chapter 7).

Demodectic Mange

Demodectic mange is a skin disease caused by mites who live in a dog's hair follicles and skin glands. If a Boston has a strong immune system, she fights off these mites. If the immune system is weak, the mites multiply and remain on the skin.

When a dog has demodectic mange, she loses hair, develops skin eruptions, and has secondary bacterial infections that itch. The coat looks moth-eaten and the skin can become bald.

Your veterinarian can diagnose mange by examining a skin scraping under a microscope. It's not contagious and the vet can prescribe a medicated dip to kill the parasites.

Skin allergies are not uncommon in Bostons. They can be hereditary.

Common Canine Problems

Just like people, even the healthiest dogs will feel a little under the weather sometimes. These are the most common canine illnesses, and what to do about them.

Appetite Loss

Bostons love to eat, but if yours misses a meal or two and is active and drinking a normal amount of water, it's probably not a problem. If she skips a third meal, has symptoms such as vomiting, diarrhea, or lethargy, or if you're concerned, contact your veterinarian.

Coughing

At least once in her life your dog will cough, and it's not a problem. Perhaps she has something caught in her throat or her throat is a little dry. If she has a persistent cough or intermittent gagging, though, she may have a respiratory infection and needs to see the veterinarian.

Diarrhea

One or two loose stools aren't serious, especially if they're followed by a normal bowel movement. Your dog may just have an upset stomach. If diarrhea continues,

Use common sense in dealing with mild upsets. If they persist for more than a day, or if your dog's behavior is worrying you, see the veterinarian.

consult your veterinarian. In a puppy, diarrhea can be the beginning of dehydration, which is serious.

The veterinarian will ask you to bring in a fresh stool sample for examination. She may prescribe an anti-diarrhea medication and suggest taking your dog off her regular diet and feeding her a bland diet consisting of rice, cottage cheese, and yogurt to settle her bowels.

Vomiting

Once in awhile your dog may vomit. Mess happens, especially if your Boston gulps too much water, has been chewing sharp blades of grass, has eaten something that doesn't agree with her, or is ill.

For one instance of vomiting, skip her next meal to give her stomach a chance to rest. Then give her a small amount of boiled rice and boiled, boneless chicken for one or two meals. If that stays down, mix in a little of her regular food by the third meal. If she vomits again, contact your veterinarian immediately.

If you have a puppy or a senior dog who vomits just twice, contact your veterinarian right away. Their systems are too fragile to wait any longer.

Basic Medical Care

Throughout your dog's life there will be times when she'll rely on you to help her recover from an illness or an accident. It helps to know how to administer to her, and that includes comforting her. You'll need to be patient and soothing so that she can relax enough to let you perform the necessary treatments.

When you have to give your Boston a pill or some liquid medication, be sure to reward her with a tasty food treat after she stands nicely for the procedure. Tell her what a great dog she is, too! You can even teach her to sit if you have to apply eye ointment or take her temperature.

Allow yourself plenty of time to take care of your dog's medical needs. Nothing is worse than having to give your dog a capsule while rushing to get ready for work.

Giving a Pill

Always ask your veterinarian if the medication can be given with food. If so, it's easy to try slipping the pill in with your dog's meal. Or, you can always disguise it. All dogs love peanut butter; crunchy or smooth both work great. Cover the capsule with some peanut butter or stuff it into a piece of string cheese or hot dog and hand it to your dog as a treat.

Does your dog spit the pill out? If so, you'll have to go to the plan B—Open Wide method. Position your dog with her back in the corner of a room or have someone hold her steady for you. Open your dog's mouth and place the pill at the back of your dog's tongue. Then quickly but gently close her mouth and tilt her head upward. Hold her mouth closed, being careful not to cover her nose, and stroke her chin. She should swallow the pill. If she spits it out again, repeat plan B.

Giving Liquid Medication

Most liquid medications come with a dropper, or your veterinarian may give you a syringe without a needle to administer the medication. Ask your veterinarian if this medication can be given with food. If so, you can mix it into your dog's next meal. If not, you'll have to lift her lips, tilt her head up slightly, and slide the dropper with the medication as far back into your dog's mouth as you can.

Squeeze the dropper slowly into her mouth. If you squirt it too fast, she may quickly spit it out. Massage beneath her chin and she'll swallow the medication.

Applying Eye Ointment

Since Bostons are prone to having eye problems, you'll no doubt be applying eye ointment to your dog's eyes a few times throughout her life. Don't worry. It's easy to do and is very soothing. She'll relax as soon as she feels it.

Hold your dog firmly and squeeze the tube slightly into the pocket between the lower lid and the eye. If she blinks, that's good. She's spreading the ointment into the eye naturally.

Those big eyes are likely to need medication at some point.

When to Call the Veterinarian

Go to the vet right away or take your dog to an emergency veterinary clinic if:

- Your dog is choking
- Your dog is having trouble breathing
- Your dog has been injured and you cannot stop the bleeding within a few minutes
- Your dog has been stung or bitten by an insect and the site is swelling
- Your dog has been bitten by a snake
- Your dog has been bitten by another animal (including a dog) and shows any swelling or bleeding
- Your dog has touched, licked, or in any way been exposed to a poison
- Your dog has been burned by either heat or caustic chemicals
- Your dog has been hit by a car
- Your dog has any obvious broken bones or cannot put any weight on one of her limbs
- Your dog has a seizure

Make an appointment to see the vet as soon as possible if:

- Your dog has been bitten by a cat, another dog, or a wild animal
- Your dog has been injured and is still limping an hour later

Taking Your Dog's Temperature

If your dog is ill, your veterinarian will ask what her temperature is. Your dog's normal rectal temperature is 100.5 to 102.5 degrees Fahrenheit. Anything higher than that is cause for concern.

It's not difficult to take a dog's temperature, nor is it painful. Feeling her ears, nose or head is not reliable. Use an oral or rectal thermometer, either digital or mercury. Ear thermometers can also be used with dogs. They are generally fast and easy, but need to be used correctly to obtain an accurate reading.

Some dogs will allow you to take their temperature, but others don't like it at all. To be on the safe side, ask someone to help you by holding your dog.

- Your dog has unexplained swelling or redness
- Your dog's appetite changes
- Your dog vomits repeatedly and can't seem to keep food down, or drools excessively while eating
- You see any changes in your dog's urination or defecation (pain during elimination, change in regular habits, blood in urine or stool, diarrhea, foul-smelling stool)
- Your dog scoots her rear end on the floor
- Your dog's energy level, attitude, or behavior changes for no apparent reason
- Your dog has crusty or cloudy eyes, or excessive tearing or discharge
- Your dog's nose is dry or chapped, hot, crusty, or runny
- Your dog's ears smell foul, have a dark discharge, or seem excessively waxy
- Your dog's gums are inflamed or bleeding, her teeth look brown, or her breath is foul
- Your dog's skin is red, flaky, itchy, or inflamed, or she keeps chewing at certain spots
- Your dog's coat is dull, dry, brittle, or bare in spots
- Your dog's paws are red, swollen, tender, cracked, or the nails are split or too long
- Your dog is panting excessively, wheezing, unable to catch her breath, breathing heavily, or sounds strange when she breathes

If you're using a mercury thermometer, shake it down first with a quick flick of the wrist until the mercury is below 94 degrees. Then lubricate the thermometer with petroleum jelly, KY jelly, or another water-based lubricant. Ask your assistant to hold your dog's head and front part of her body steady.

Lift the tail and insert the thermometer slowly and carefully into the rectum, located just below the base of the tail. Insert the thermometer about one inch and hold in place—two minutes for mercury thermometers or until the digital thermometer beeps.

Remove the thermometer and read the temperature. Write down the results so you won't forget what it was when you call the veterinarian.

It's an Emergency

If your dog has any of these conditions, wrap her in a blanket if she can't move and take her to the emergency clinic immediately. Call ahead to let the clinic know you are on the way.

Broken Bone

Ouch! Your dog has run into something or has twisted a leg. If she has a broken bone, you'll probably know it. She won't be able to move the leg or stand up and walk, and she'll be holding the injured leg up off the ground. If you touch it, she'll likely yelp in pain. Chances are it's also dangling or severely swollen.

Take her to the emergency clinic immediately. Don't try to wrap it in a splint and don't wait!

Choking

Leave it to a Boston Terrier to chew up something she's not supposed to! In the process of gnawing a foreign object, it can easily become lodged in her throat.

If you see your dog gagging, pawing at her mouth, rubbing her face on the ground, or having difficulty swallowing or breathing, she's choking. Carefully open her mouth to find out if there's something you can easily remove. If you can't see anything, take your dog to the emergency clinic immediately.

Overheating is a major concern. Keep your dog quiet and cool in the warm weather.

Heatstroke

One of the major dangers facing Bostons is heatstroke. Because of their dark coats and shortened muzzles, they have a greater tendency than other breeds to overheat in warm weather. Heatstroke occurs when the body's ability to release heat cannot keep up with the high temperature of the air around the body. The dog may breathe rapidly or pant loudly. She may become disoriented and stagger, vomit, collapse, or have a seizure. Heatstroke can be fatal.

You can prevent heatstroke by keeping your Boston indoors and

How to Make a Canine First-Aid Kit

If your dog hurts herself, even a minor cut, it can be very upsetting for both of you. Having a first-aid kit handy will help you to help her, calmly and efficiently. What should be in your canine first-aid kit?

- Antibiotic ointment
- Antiseptic and antibacterial cleansing wipes
- Benadryl
- Cotton-tipped applicators
- Disposable razor
- Elastic wrap bandages
- Extra leash and collar
- First-aid tape of various widths
- Gauze bandage roll
- Gauze pads of different sizes, including eye pads
- Hydrogen peroxide
- Instant cold compress
- Kaopectate tablets or liquid
- Latex gloves
- Lubricating jelly
- Muzzle
- Nail clippers
- Pen, pencil, and paper for notes and directions
- Pepto-Bismol
- Round-ended scissors and pointy scissors
- Safety pins
- Sterile saline eyewash
- Thermometer (rectal)
- Tweezers

cool during warm weather, avoiding hot cars, and taking plenty of cool water and ice with you if you must be out and about in warmer weather. Do not allow your Boston to exercise vigorously or to remain outdoors in extreme heat.

If your Boston overheats, get her to a cool location in the shade as quickly as possible. Bathe her in cool (not ice cold) water and turn a fan on her to evaporate the water and cool her body. Take her temperature with a rectal thermometer. If it is at all higher than normal, continue your attempts to cool her down as you transport her to your veterinarian or the nearest emergency hospital.

ASPCA Animal Poison Control Center

The ASPCA Animal Poison Control Center has a staff of licensed veterinarians and board-certified toxicologists available 24 hours a day, 365 days a year. The number to call is (888) 426-4435. You will be charged a consultation fee of $50 per case, charged to most major credit cards. There is no charge for follow-up calls in critical cases. At your request, they will also contact your veterinarian. Specific treatment and information can be provided via fax. Put the number in large, legible print with your other emergency telephone numbers. Be prepared to give your name, address, and phone number; what your dog has gotten into (the amount and how long ago); your dog's breed, age, sex, and weight; and what signs and symptoms the dog is showing. You can log onto www.aspca.org and click on "Animal Poison Control Center" for more information, including a list of toxic and nontoxic plants.

Your dog is counting on you to know what to do in an emergency.

Insect Stings

If you've ever had a bee sting, you know that it can hurt. In dogs who are allergic to bee stings or other insects, it can be fatal. Allergic reactions include hives or swelling around the mouth, face, and body, and breathing difficulties. Try to keep your dog as calm as possible, because that will prevent the reaction from getting any worse. If necessary, attach her leash to her collar so that she can't run around.

If you see the stinger, remove it with a pair of tweezers. Dab the area with alcohol and cold water. Call your veterinarian immediately. She may suggest an anti-inflammatory ointment or cream or an antihistamine until you can get your dog to the vet's office.

Poisoning

If your Boston inhales or ingests a poisonous substance, she may show signs of having a seizure, vomiting, or having trouble breathing. Diarrhea, pain, and foul-smelling body or breath odor are other signs of poisoning.

Call the ASPCA Animal Poison Control Center hotline (see the box on page 100), then take your Boston to your veterinarian or emergency clinic immediately!

Shock

A dog will go into shock after having an accident and experiencing a severe trauma, such as poisoning, loss of blood, second- or third-degree burns, dehydration, or infection.

Shock can range from mild to life-threatening, and will cause a dog to have labored breathing, a vacant, glassy-eyed look, feel extremely weak, and be cold to the touch. Instead of being the healthy, normal pink color, her gums will be beige.

No doubt you'll be frightened when you see your dog in shock, but remember to keep her warm with a blanket or a towel and try to remain as calm as possible. If you're calm, she'll be, too. Transport her to the veterinarian right away.

Bees, spiders, and other bugs in your garden can give your dog a nasty bite or sting.

Part III

Enjoying Your Boston Terrier

Chapter 9

Training Your Boston Terrier

by Peggy Moran

Training makes your best friend better! A properly trained dog has a happier life and a longer life expectancy. He is also more appreciated by the people he encounters each day, both at home and out and about.

A trained dog walks nicely and joins his family often, going places untrained dogs cannot go. He is never rude or unruly, and he always happily comes when called. When he meets people for the first time, he greets them by sitting and waiting to be petted, rather than jumping up. At home he doesn't compete with his human family, and alone he is not destructive or overly anxious. He isn't continually nagged with words like "no," since he has learned not to misbehave in the first place. He is never shamed, harshly punished, or treated unkindly, and he is a well-loved, involved member of the family.

Sounds good, doesn't it? If you are willing to invest some time, thought, and patience, the words above could soon be used to describe your dog (though perhaps changing "he" to "she"). Educating your pet in a positive way is fun and easy, and there is no better gift you can give your pet than the guarantee of improved understanding and a great relationship.

This chapter will explain how to offer kind leadership, reshape your pet's behavior in a positive and practical way, and even get a head start on simple obedience training.

Understanding Builds the Bond

Dog training is a learning adventure on both ends of the leash. Before attempting to teach their dog new behaviors or change unwanted ones, thoughtful dog owners take the time to understand why their pets behave the way they do, and how their own behavior can be either a positive or negative influence on their dog.

Canine Nature

Loving dogs as much as we do, it's easy to forget they are a completely different species. Despite sharing our homes and living as appreciated members of our families, dogs do not think or learn exactly the same way people do. Even if you love your dog like a child, you must remember to respect the fact that he is actually a dog.

Dogs have no idea when their behavior is inappropriate from a human perspective. They are not aware of the value of possessions they chew or of messes they make or the worry they sometimes seem to cause. While people tend to look at behavior as good and bad or right and wrong, dogs just discover what works and what doesn't work. Then they behave accordingly, learning from their own experiences and increasing or reducing behaviors to improve results for themselves.

You might wonder, "But don't dogs want to please us"? My answer is yes, provided your pleasure reflects back to them in positive ways they can feel and appreciate. Dogs do things for *dog* reasons, and everything they do works for them in some way or they wouldn't be doing it!

The Social Dog

Our pets descended from animals who lived in tightly knit, cooperative social groups. Though far removed in appearance and lifestyle from their ancestors, our dogs still relate in many of the same ways their wild relatives did. And in their relationships with one another, wild canids either lead or follow.

Canine ranking relationships are not about cruelty and power; they are about achievement and abilities. Competent dogs with high levels of drive and confidence step up, while deferring dogs step aside. But followers don't get the short end of the stick; they benefit from the security of having a more competent dog at the helm.

Our domestic dogs still measure themselves against other members of their group—us! Dog owners whose actions lead to positive results have willing, secure followers. But dogs may step up and fill the void or cut loose and do their own thing when their people fail to show capable leadership. When dogs are pushy, aggressive, and rude, or independent and unwilling, it's not because they have designs on the role of "master." It is more likely their owners failed to provide consistent leadership.

Dogs in training benefit from their handler's good leadership. Their education flows smoothly because they are impressed. Being in charge doesn't require you to physically dominate or punish your dog. You simply need to make some subtle changes in the way you relate to him every day.

Lead Your Pack!

Create schedules and structure daily activities. Dogs are creatures of habit and routines will create security. Feed meals at the same times each day and also try to schedule regular walks, training practices, and toilet outings. Your predictability will help your dog be patient.

Ask your dog to perform a task. Before releasing him to food or freedom, have him do something as simple as sit on command. Teach him that cooperation earns great results!

Give a release prompt (such as "let's go") when going through doors leading outside. This is a better idea than allowing your impatient pup to rush past you.

Pet your dog when he is calm, not when he is excited. Turn your touch into a tool that relaxes and settles.

Reward desirable rather than inappropriate behavior. Petting a jumping dog (who hasn't been invited up) reinforces jumping. Pet sitting dogs, and only invite lap dogs up after they've first "asked" by waiting for your invitation.

Replace personal punishment with positive reinforcement. Show a dog what *to do,* and motivate him to want to do it, and there will be no need to punish him for what he should *not do.* Dogs naturally follow, without the need for force or harshness.

Play creatively and appropriately. Your dog will learn the most about his social rank when he is playing with you. During play, dogs work to control toys and try to get the best of one another in a friendly way. The wrong sorts of play can create problems: For example, tug of war can lead to aggressiveness. Allowing your dog to control toys during play may result in possessive guarding when he has something he really values, such as a bone. Dogs who are chased during play may later run away from you when you approach to leash them. The right kinds of play will help increase your dog's social confidence while you gently assert your leadership.

How Dogs Learn (and How They Don't)

Dog training begins as a meeting of minds—yours and your dog's. Though the end goal may be to get your dog's body to behave in a specific way, training starts as a mind game. Your dog is learning all the time by observing the consequences of his actions and social interactions. He is always seeking out what he perceives as desirable and trying to avoid what he perceives as undesirable.

He will naturally repeat a behavior that either brings him more good stuff or makes bad stuff go away (these are both types of reinforcement). He will naturally avoid a behavior that brings him more bad stuff or makes the good stuff go away (these are both types of punishment).

Both reinforcement and punishment can be perceived as either the direct result of something the dog did himself, or as coming from an outside source.

Using Life's Rewards

Your best friend is smart and he is also cooperative. When the best things in life can only be had by working with you, your dog will view you as a facilitator. You unlock doors to all of the positively reinforcing experiences he values: his freedom, his friends at the park, food, affection, walks, and play. The trained dog accompanies you through those doors and waits to see what working with you will bring.

Rewarding your dog for good behavior is called positive reinforcement, and, as we've just seen, it increases the likelihood that he will repeat that behavior. The perfect reward is anything your dog wants that is safe and appropriate. Don't limit yourself to toys, treats, and things that come directly from you. Harness life's positives—barking at squirrels, chasing a falling leaf, bounding away from you at the dog park, pausing for a moment to sniff everything—and allow your dog to earn access to those things as rewards that come from cooperating with you. When he looks at you, when he sits, when he comes when you call—any prompted behavior can earn one of life's rewards. When he works with you, he earns the things he most appreciates; but when he tries to get those things on his own, he cannot. Rather than seeing you as someone who always says "no," your dog will view you as the one who says "let's go!" He will *want* to follow.

What About Punishment?

Not only is it unnecessary to personally punish dogs, it is abusive. No matter how convinced you are that your dog "knows right from wrong," in reality he will associate personal punishment with the punisher. The resulting cowering, "guilty"-looking postures are actually displays of submission and fear. Later,

Purely Positive Reinforcement

With positive training, we emphasize teaching dogs what they should do to earn reinforcements, rather than punishing them for unwanted behaviors.

- Focus on teaching "do" rather than "don't." For example, a sitting dog isn't jumping.
- Use positive reinforcers that are valuable to your dog and the situation: A tired dog values rest; a confined dog values freedom.
- Play (appropriately)!
- Be a consistent leader.
- Set your dog up for success by anticipating and preventing problems.
- Notice and reward desirable behavior, and give him lots of attention when he is being good.
- Train ethically. Use humane methods and equipment that do not frighten or hurt your dog.
- When you are angry, walk away and plan a positive strategy.
- Keep practice sessions short and sweet. Five to ten minutes, three to five times a day is best.

when the punisher isn't around and the coast is clear, the same behavior he was punished for—such as raiding a trash can—might bring a self-delivered, very tasty result. The punished dog hasn't learned not to misbehave; he has learned to not get caught.

Does punishment ever have a place in dog training? Many people will heartily insist it does not. But dog owners often get frustrated as they try to stick to the path of all-positive reinforcement. It sure sounds great, but is it realistic, or even natural, to *never* say "no" to your dog?

A wild dog's life is not *all* positive. Hunger and thirst are both examples of negative reinforcement; the resulting discomfort motivates the wild dog to seek food and water. He encounters natural aversives such as pesky insects; mats in his coat; cold days; rainy days; sweltering hot days; and occasional run-ins with thorns, brambles, skunks, bees, and other nastiness. These all affect his behavior, as he tries to avoid the bad stuff whenever possible. The wild dog also occasionally encounters social punishers from others in his group when he gets too pushy. Starting with a growl or a snap from Mom, and later some mild and ritualized discipline from other members of his four-legged family, he learns to modify behaviors that elicit grouchy responses.

Our pet dogs don't naturally experience all positive results either, because they learn from their surroundings and from social experiences with other dogs. Watch a group of pet dogs playing together and you'll see a very old educational system still being used. As they wrestle and attempt to assert themselves, you'll notice many mouth-on-neck moments. Their playful biting is inhibited, with no intention to cause harm, but their message is clear: "Say uncle or this could hurt more!"

Observing that punishment does occur in nature, some people may feel compelled to try to be like the big wolf with their pet dogs. Becoming aggressive or heavy-handed with your pet will backfire! Your dog will not be impressed, nor will he want to follow you. Punishment causes dogs to change their behavior to avoid or escape discomfort and threats. Threatened dogs will either become very passive and offer submissive, appeasing postures, attempt to flee, or rise to the occasion and fight back. When people personally punish their dogs in an angry manner, one of these three defensive mechanisms will be triggered. Which one depends on a dog's genetic temperament as well as his past social experiences. Since we don't want to make our pets feel the need to avoid or escape us, personal punishment has no place in our training.

Remote Consequences

Sometimes, however, all-positive reinforcement is just not enough. That's because not all reinforcement comes from us. An inappropriate behavior can be self-reinforcing—just doing it makes the dog feel better in some way, whether you are there to say "good boy!" or not. Some examples are eating garbage, pulling the stuffing out of your sofa, barking at passersby, or urinating on the floor.

Although you don't want to personally punish your dog, the occasional deterrent may be called for to help derail these kinds of self-rewarding misbehaviors. In these cases, mild forms of impersonal or remote punishment can be used as part of a correction. The goal isn't to make your dog feel bad or to "know he has done wrong," but to help redirect him to alternate behaviors that are more acceptable to you.

The Problems with Personal Punishment

- Personally punished dogs are not taught appropriate behaviors.
- Personally punished dogs only stop misbehaving when they are caught or interrupted, but they don't learn not to misbehave when they are alone.
- Personally punished dogs become shy, fearful, and distrusting.
- Personally punished dogs may become defensively aggressive.
- Personally punished dogs become suppressed and inhibited.
- Personally punished dogs become stressed, triggering stress-reducing behaviors that their owners interpret as acts of spite, triggering even more punishment.
- Personally punished dogs have stressed owners.
- Personally punished dogs may begin to repeat behaviors they have been taught will result in negative, but predictable, attention.
- Personally punished dogs are more likely to be given away than are positively trained dogs.

You do this by pairing a slightly startling, totally impersonal sound with an equally impersonal and *very mild* remote consequence. The impersonal sound might be a single shake of an empty plastic pop bottle with pennies in it, held out of your dog's sight. Or you could use a vocal expression such as "eh!" delivered with you looking *away* from your misbehaving dog.

Pair your chosen sound—the penny bottle or "eh!"—with either a slight tug on his collar or a sneaky spritz on the rump from a water bottle. Do this right *as* he touches something he should not; bad timing will confuse your dog and undermine your training success.

To keep things under your control and make sure you get the timing right, it's best to do this as a setup. "Accidentally" drop a shoe on the floor, and then help your dog learn some things are best avoided. As he sniffs the shoe say "eh!" without looking at him and give a *slight* tug against his collar. This sound will quickly become meaningful as a correction all by itself—sometimes after just one setup—making the tug correction obsolete. The tug lets your dog see that you were right; going for that shoe *was* a bad idea! Your wise dog will be more likely to heed your warning next time, and probably move closer to you where it's safe. Be a good friend and pick up the nasty shoe. He'll be relieved and you'll look heroic. Later, when he's home alone and encounters a stray shoe, he'll want to give it a wide berth.

Your negative marking sound will come in handy in the future, when your dog begins to venture down the wrong behavioral path. The goal is not to announce your disapproval or to threaten your dog. You are not telling him to stop or showing how *you* feel about his behavior. You are sounding a warning to a friend who's venturing off toward danger—"I wouldn't if I were you!" Suddenly, there is an abrupt, rather startling, noise! Now is the moment to redirect him and help him earn positive reinforcement. That interrupted behavior will become something he wants to avoid in the future, but he won't want to avoid you.

Practical Commands for Family Pets

Before you begin training your dog, let's look at some equipment you'll want to have on hand:

- **A buckle collar** is fine for most dogs. If your dog pulls *very* hard, try a head collar, a device similar to a horse halter that helps reduce pulling by turning the dog's head. *Do not* use a choke chain (sometimes called a training collar), because they cause physical harm even when used correctly.
- **Six-foot training leash and a longer line that you can make from sturdy nylon cord.**
- **A few empty plastic soda bottles with about twenty pennies in each one.** This will be used to impersonally interrupt misbehaviors before redirecting dogs to more positive activities.
- **A favorite squeaky toy,** to motivate, attract attention, and reward your dog during training.

Lure your dog to take just a few steps with you on the leash by being inviting and enthusiastic. Make sure you reward him for his efforts.

Baby Steps

Allow your young pup to drag a short, lightweight leash attached to a buckle collar for a few *supervised* moments, several times each day. At first the leash may annoy him and he may jump around a bit trying to get away from it. Distract him with your squeaky toy or a bit of his kibble and he'll quickly get used to his new "tail."

Begin walking him on the leash by holding the end and following him. As he adapts, you can begin to assert gentle direct pressure to teach him to follow you. Don't jerk or yank, or he will become afraid to walk when the leash is on. If he becomes hesitant, squat down facing him and let him figure out that by moving toward you he is safe and secure. If he remains confused or frightened and doesn't come to you, go to him and help him understand that you provide safe harbor while he's on the leash. Then back away a few steps and try again to lure him to you. As he learns that you are the "home base," he'll want to follow when you walk a few steps, waiting for you to stop, squat down, and make him feel great.

So Attached to You!

The next step in training your dog—and this is a very important one—is to begin spending at least an hour or more each day with him on a four- to six-foot leash, held by or tethered to you. This training will increase his attachment to you—literally!—as you sit quietly or walk about, tending to your household business. When you are quiet, he'll learn it is time to settle; when you are active, he'll learn to move with you. Tethering also keeps him out of trouble when you are busy but still want his company. It is a great alternative to confining a dog, and can be used instead of crating any time you're home and need to slow him down a bit.

Rotating your dog from supervised freedom to tethered time to some quiet time in the crate or his gated area gives him a diverse and balanced day while he is learning. Two confined or tethered hours is the most you should require of your dog in one stretch, before changing to some supervised freedom, play, or a walk.

The dog in training may, at times, be stressed by all of the changes he is dealing with. Provide a stress outlet, such as a toy to chew on, when he is confined or tethered. He will settle into his quiet time more quickly and completely. Always be sure to provide several rounds of daily play and free time (in a fenced area or on your long line) in addition to plenty of chewing materials.

Dog Talk

Dogs don't speak in words, but they do have a language—body language. They use postures, vocalizations, movements, facial gestures,

Tethering your dog is great way to keep him calm and under control, but still with you.

odors, and touch—usually with their mouths—to communicate what they are feeling and thinking.

We also "speak" using body language. We have quite an array of postures, movements, and facial gestures that accompany our touch and language as we attempt to communicate with our pets. And our dogs can quickly figure us out!

Alone, without associations, words are just noises. But, because we pair them with meaningful body language, our dogs make the connection. Dogs can really learn to understand much of what we *say*, if what we *do* at the same time is consistent.

The Positive Marker

Start your dog's education with one of the best tricks in dog training: Pair various positive reinforcers—food, a toy, touch—with a sound such as a click on a clicker (which you can get at the pet supply store) or a spoken word like "good!" or "yes!" This will enable you to later "mark" your dog's desirable behaviors.

It seems too easy: Just say "yes!" and give the dog his toy. (Or use whatever sound and reward you have chosen.) Later, when you make your marking sound right at the instant your dog does the right thing, he will know you are going to be giving him something good for that particular action. And he'll be eager to repeat the behavior to hear you mark it again!

Next, you must teach your dog to understand the meaning of cues you'll be using to ask him to perform specific behaviors. This is easy, too. Does he already do things you might like him to do on command? Of course! He lies down, he sits, he picks things up, he drops them again, he comes to you. All of the behaviors you'd like to control are already part of your dog's natural repertoire. The trick is getting him to offer those behaviors when you ask for them. And that means you have to teach him to associate a particular behavior on his part with a particular behavior on your part.

Sit Happens

Teach your dog an important new rule: From now on, he is only touched and petted when he is either sitting or lying down. You won't need to ask him to sit; in fact, you should not. Just keeping him tethered near you so there isn't much to do but stand, be ignored, or settle, and wait until sit happens.

He may pester you a bit, but be stoic and unresponsive. Starting now, when *you* are sitting down, a sitting dog is the only one you see and pay attention to. He will eventually sit, and as he does, attach the word "sit"—but don't be too excited or he'll jump right back up. Now mark with your positive sound that promises something good, then reward him with a slow, quiet, settling pet.

Training requires consistent reinforcement. Ask others to also wait until your dog is sitting and calm to touch him, and he will associate being petted with being relaxed. Be sure you train your dog to associate everyone's touch with quiet bonding.

Reinforcing "Sit" as a Command

Since your dog now understands one concept of working for a living—sit to earn petting—you can begin to shape and reinforce his desire to sit. Hold toys, treats, his bowl of food, and turn into a statue. But don't prompt him to sit! Instead, remain frozen and unavailable, looking somewhere out into space, over his head. He will put on a bit of a show, trying to get a response from you, and may offer various behaviors, but only one will push your button—sitting. Wait for him to offer the "right" behavior, and when he does, you unfreeze. Say "sit," then mark with an excited "good!" and give him the toy or treat with a release command—"OK!"

When you notice spontaneous sits occurring, be sure to take advantage of those free opportunities to make your command sequence meaningful and positive. Say "sit" as you observe sit happen—then mark with "good!" and praise, pet, or reward the dog. Soon, every time you look at your dog he'll be sitting and looking right back at you!

Now, after thirty days of purely positive practice, it's time to give him a test. When he is just walking around doing his own thing, suddenly ask him to sit. He'll probably do it right away. If he doesn't, do *not* repeat your command, or you'll just undermine its meaning ("sit" means sit *now;* the command is not "sit, sit, sit, sit"). Instead, get something he likes and let him know you have it. Wait for him to offer the sit—he will—then say "sit!" and complete your marking and rewarding sequence.

OK

"OK" will probably rate as one of your dog's favorite words. It's like the word "recess" to schoolchildren. It is the word used to release your dog from a command. You can introduce "OK" during your "sit" practice. When he gets up from a sit, say "OK" to tell him the sitting is finished. Soon that sound will mean "freedom."

Make it even more meaningful and positive. Whenever he spontaneously bounds away, say "OK!" Squeak a toy, and when he notices and shows interest, toss it for him.

Down

I've mentioned that you should only pet your dog when he is either sitting or lying down. Now, using the approach I've just introduced for "sit," teach your dog to lie down. You will be a statue, and hold something he would like to get but that you'll only release to a dog who is lying down. It helps to lower the desired item to the floor in front of him, still not speaking and not letting him have it until he offers you the new behavior you are seeking.

Lower your dog's reward to the floor to help him figure out what behavior will earn him his reward.

He may offer a sit and then wait expectantly, but you must make him keep searching for the new trick that triggers your generosity. Allow your dog to experiment and find the right answer, even if he has to search around for it first. When he lands on "down" and learns it is another behavior that works, he'll offer it more quickly the next time.

Don't say "down" until he lies down, to tightly associate your prompt with the correct behavior. To say "down, down, down" as he is sitting, looking at you, or pawing at the toy would make "down" mean those behaviors instead! Whichever behavior he offers, a training opportunity has been created. Once you've attached and shaped both sitting and lying down, you can ask for both behaviors with your verbal prompts, "sit" or "down." Be sure to only reinforce the "correct" reply!

Stay

"Stay" can easily be taught as an extension of what you've already been practicing. To teach "stay," you follow the entire sequence for reinforcing a "sit" or "down," except you wait a bit longer before you give the release word, "OK!" Wait a second or two longer during each practice before saying "OK!" and releasing your dog to the positive reinforcer (toy, treat, or one of life's other rewards).

You can step on the leash to help your dog understand the down-stay, but only do this when he is already lying down. You don't want to hurt him!

If he gets up before you've said "OK," you have two choices: pretend the release was your idea and quickly interject "OK!" as he breaks; or, if he is more experienced and practiced, mark the behavior with your correction sound— "eh!"—and then gently put him back on the spot, wait for him to lie down, and begin again. Be sure the next three practices are a success. Ask him to wait for just a second, and release him before he can be wrong. You need to keep your dog feeling like more of a success than a failure as you begin to test his training in increasingly more distracting and difficult situations.

As he gets the hang of it—he stays until you say "OK"— you can gradually push for longer times—up to a minute on a sit-stay, and up to three minutes on a down-stay. You can also gradually add distractions and work in new environments. To add a minor self-correction for the down-stay, stand on the dog's leash after he lies down, allowing about three inches of slack. If tries to get up before you've said "OK," he'll discover it doesn't work.

Do not step on the leash to make your dog lie down! This could badly hurt his neck, and will destroy his trust in you. Remember, we are teaching our dogs to make the best choices, not inflicting our answers upon them!

Come

Rather than thinking of "come" as an action—"come to me"—think of it as a place—"the dog is sitting in front of me, facing me." Since your dog by now really likes sitting to earn your touch and other positive reinforcement, he's likely to sometimes sit directly in front of you, facing you, all on his own. When this happens, give it a specific name: "come."

Now follow the rest of the training steps you have learned to make him like doing it and reinforce the behavior by practicing it any chance you get. Anything your dog wants and likes could be earned as a result of his first offering the sit-in-front known as "come."

You can help guide him into the right location. Use your hands as "landing gear" and pat the insides of your legs at his nose level. Do this while backing up a bit, to help him maneuver to the straight-in-front, facing-you position. Don't say the

Pat the insides of your legs to show your dog exactly where you like him to sit when you say "come."

word "come" while he's maneuvering, because he hasn't! You are trying to make "come" the end result, not the work in progress.

You can also help your dog by marking his movement in the right direction: Use your positive sound or word to promise he is getting warm. When he finally sits facing you, enthusiastically say "come," mark again with your positive word, and release him with an enthusiastic "OK!" Make it so worth his while, with lots of play and praise, that he can't wait for you to ask him to come again!

Building a Better Recall

Practice, practice, practice. Now, practice some more. Teach your dog that all good things in life hinge upon him first sitting in front of you in a behavior named "come." When you think he really has got it, test him by asking him to "come" as you gradually add distractions and change locations. Expect setbacks as you make these changes and practice accordingly. Lower your expectations and make his task easier so he is able to get it right. Use those distractions as rewards, when they are appropriate. For example, let him check out the interesting leaf that blew by as a reward for first coming to you and ignoring it.

Add distance and call your dog to come while he is on his long line. If he refuses and sits looking at you blankly, *do not* jerk, tug, "pop," or reel him in. Do nothing! It is his move; wait to see what behavior he offers. He'll either begin to approach (mark the behavior with an excited "good!"), sit and do nothing (just keep waiting), or he'll try to move in some direction other than toward you. If he tries to leave, use your correction marker—"eh!"— and bring him to a stop by letting him walk to the end of the leash, *not* by jerking him. Now walk to him in a neutral manner, and don't jerk or show any disapproval. Gently bring him back to the spot where he was when you called him, then back away and face him, still waiting and not reissuing your command. Let him keep examining his options until he finds the one that works—yours!

If you have practiced everything I've suggested so far and given your dog a chance to really learn what "come" means, he is well aware of what you want and is quite intelligently weighing all his options. The only way he'll know your way is the one that works is to be allowed to examine his other choices and discover that they *don't* work.

Sooner or later every dog tests his training. Don't be offended or angry when your dog tests you. No matter how positive you've made it, he won't always want to do everything you ask, every time. When he explores the "what happens if I don't" scenario, your training is being strengthened. He will discover through his own process of trial and error that the best—and only—way out of a command he really doesn't feel compelled to obey is to obey it.

Let's Go

Many pet owners wonder if they can retain control while walking their dogs and still allow at least some running in front, sniffing, and playing. You might worry that allowing your dog occasional freedom could result in him expecting it all the time, leading to a testy, leash-straining walk. It's possible for both parties on the leash to have an enjoyable experience by implementing and reinforcing well-thought-out training techniques.

Begin by making word associations you'll use on your walks. Give the dog some slack on the leash, and as he starts to walk away from you say "OK" and begin to follow him.

Do not let him drag you; set the pace even when he is being given a turn at being the leader. Whenever he starts to pull, just come to a standstill and refuse to move (or refuse to allow him to continue forward) until there is slack in the leash. Do this correction without saying anything at all. When he isn't pulling, you may decide to just stand still and let him sniff about within the range the slack leash allows, or you may even mosey along following him. After a few minutes of "recess," it is time to work. Say something like "that's it" or "time's up," close the distance between you and your dog, and touch him.

Next say "let's go" (or whatever command you want to use to mean "follow me as we walk"). Turn and walk off, and, if he follows, mark his behavior with "good!" Then stop,

Give your dog slack on his leash as you walk and let him make the decision to walk with you.

When your dog catches up with you, make sure you let him know what a great dog he is!

Intersperse periods of attentive walking, where your dog is on a shorter leash, with periods on a slack leash, where he is allowed to look and sniff around.

squat down, and let him catch you. Make him glad he did! Start again, and do a few transitions as he gets the hang of your follow-the-leader game, speeding up, slowing down, and trying to make it fun. When you stop, he gets to catch up and receive some deserved positive reinforcement. Don't forget that's the reason he is following you, so be sure to make it worth his while!

Require him to remain attentive to you. Do not allow sniffing, playing, eliminating, or pulling during your time as leader on a walk. If he seems to get distracted—which, by the way, is the main reason dogs walk poorly with their people—change direction or pace without saying a word. Just help him realize "oops, I lost track of my human." Do not jerk his neck and say "heel"—this will make the word "heel" mean pain in the neck and will not encourage him to cooperate with you. Don't repeat "let's go," either. He needs to figure out that it is his job to keep track of and follow you if he wants to earn the positive benefits you provide.

The best reward you can give a dog for performing an attentive, controlled walk is a few minutes of walking without all of the controls. Of course, he must remain on a leash even during the "recess" parts of the walk, but allowing him to discriminate between attentive following—"let's go"—and having a few moments of relaxation—"OK"—will increase his willingness to work.

Training for Attention

Your dog pretty much has a one-track mind. Once he is focused on something, everything else is excluded. This can be great, for instance, when he's focusing on you! But it can also be dangerous if, for example, his attention is riveted on the bunny he is chasing and he does not hear you call—that is, not unless he has been trained to pay attention when you say his name.

When you say your dog's name, you'll want him to make eye contact with you. Begin teaching this by making yourself so intriguing that he can't help but look.

When you call your dog's name, you will again be seeking a specific response—eye contact. The best way to teach this is to trigger his alerting response by making a noise with your mouth, such as whistling or a kissing sound, and then immediately doing something he'll find very intriguing.

You can play a treasure hunt game to help teach him to regard his name as a request for attention. As a bonus, you can reinforce the rest of his new vocabulary at the same time.

Treasure Hunt

Make a kissing sound, then jump up and find a dog toy or dramatically raid the fridge and rather noisily eat a piece of cheese. After doing this twice, make a kissing sound and then look at your dog.

Of course he is looking at you! He is waiting to see if that sound—the kissing sound—means you're going to go hunting again. After all, you're so good at it! Because he is looking, say his name, mark with "good," then go hunting and find his toy. Release it to him with an "OK." At any point if he follows you, attach your "let's go!" command; if he leaves you, give permission with "OK."

Using this approach, he cannot be wrong—any behavior your dog offers can be named. You can add things like "take it" when he picks up a toy, and "thank you" when he happens to drop one. Many opportunities to make your new vocabulary meaningful and positive can be found within this simple training game.

Problems to watch out for when teaching the treasure hunt:

- You really do not want your dog to come to you when you call his name (later, when you try to engage his attention to ask him to stay, he'll already be on his way toward you). You just want him to look at you.
- Saying "watch me, watch me" doesn't teach your dog to *offer* his attention. It just makes you a background noise.
- Don't lure your dog's attention with the reward. Get his attention and then reward him for looking. Try holding a toy in one hand with your arm stretched out to your side. Wait until he looks at you rather than the toy. Now say his name then mark with "good!" and release the toy. As he goes for it, say "OK."

To get your dog's attention, try holding his toy with your arm out to your side. Wait until he looks at you, then mark the moment and give him the toy.

Teaching Cooperation

Never punish your dog for failing to obey you or try to punish him into compliance. Bribing, repeating yourself, and doing a behavior for him all avoid the real issue of dog training—his will. He must be helped to be willing, not made to achieve tasks. Good dog training helps your dog want to obey. He learns that he can gain what he values most through cooperation and compliance, and can't gain those things any other way.

Your dog is learning to *earn*, rather than expect, the good things in life. And you've become much more important to him than you were before. Because you are allowing him to experiment and learn, he doesn't have to be forced, manipulated, or bribed. When he wants something, he can gain it by cooperating with you. One of those "somethings"—and a great reward you shouldn't underestimate—is your positive attention, paid to him with love and sincere approval!

Chapter 10

Housetraining Your Boston Terrier

Excerpted from Housetraining: An Owner's Guide to a Happy Healthy Pet, 1st Edition, *by September Morn*

By the time puppies are about 3 weeks old, they start to follow their mother around. When they are a few steps away from their clean sleeping area, the mama dog stops. The pups try to nurse but mom won't allow it. The pups mill around in frustration, then nature calls and they all urinate and defecate here, away from their bed. The mother dog returns to the nest, with her brood waddling behind her. Their first housetraining lesson has been a success.

The next one to housetrain puppies should be their breeder. The breeder watches as the puppies eliminate, then deftly removes the soiled papers and replaces them with clean papers before the pups can traipse back through their messes. He has wisely arranged the puppies' space so their bed, food, and drinking water are as far away from the elimination area as possible. This way, when the pups follow their mama, they will move away from their sleeping and eating area before eliminating. This habit will help the pups be easily housetrained.

Your Housetraining Shopping List

While your puppy's mother and breeder are getting her started on good housetraining habits, you'll need to do some shopping. If you have all the essentials in place before your dog arrives, it will be easier to help her learn the rules from day one.

Newspaper: The younger your puppy and larger her breed, the more newspapers you'll need. Newspaper is absorbent, abundant, cheap, and convenient.

Puddle Pads: If you prefer not to stockpile newspaper, a commercial alternative is puddle pads. These thick paper pads can be purchased under several trade names at pet supply stores. The pads have waterproof backing, so puppy urine doesn't seep through onto the floor. Their disadvantages are that they will cost you more than newspapers and that they contain plastics that are not biodegradable.

Poop Removal Tool: There are several types of poop removal tools available. Some are designed with a separate pan and rake, and others have the handles hinged like scissors. Some scoops need two hands for operation, while others are designed for one-handed use. Try out the different brands at your pet supply store. Put a handful of pebbles or dog kibble on the floor and then pick them up with each type of scoop to determine which works best for you.

Plastic Bags: When you take your dog outside your yard, you *must* pick up after her. Dog waste is unsightly, smelly, and can harbor disease. In many cities and towns, the law mandates dog owners clean up pet waste deposited on public ground. Picking up after your dog using a plastic bag scoop is simple. Just put your hand inside the bag, like a mitten,

Housetraining is a matter of establishing good habits right from the start. The very first day, take your puppy to her elimination spot and praise her when she goes.

and then grab the droppings. Turn the bag inside out, tie the top, and that's that.

Crate: To housetrain a puppy, you will need some way to confine her when you're unable to supervise. A dog crate is a secure way to confine your dog for short periods during the day and to use as a comfortable bed at night. Crates come in wire mesh and in plastic. The wire ones are foldable to store flat in a smaller space. The plastic ones are more cozy, draftfree, and quiet, and are approved for airline travel.

Baby Gates: Since you shouldn't crate a dog for more than an hour or two at a time during the day, baby gates are a good way to limit your dog's freedom in the house. Be sure the baby gates you use are safe. The old-fashioned wooden, expanding lattice type has seriously injured a number of children by collapsing and trapping a leg, arm, or neck. That type of gate can hurt a puppy, too, so use the modern grid type gates instead. You'll need more than one baby gate if you have several doorways to close off.

Exercise Pen: Portable exercise pens are great when you have a young pup or a small dog. These metal or plastic pens are made of rectangular panels that are hinged together. The pens are freestanding, sturdy, foldable, and can be carried like a suitcase. You could set one up in your kitchen as the pup's daytime corral, and then take it outdoors to contain your pup while you garden or just sit and enjoy the day.

Enzymatic Cleaner: All dogs make housetraining mistakes. Accept this and be ready for it by buying an enzymatic cleaner made especially for pet accidents. Dogs like to eliminate where they have done it before, and lingering smells lead them to those spots. Ordinary household cleaners may remove all the odors you can smell, but only an enzymatic cleaner will remove everything your dog can smell.

The First Day

Housetraining is a matter of establishing good habits in your dog. That means you never want her to learn anything she will eventually have to unlearn. Start off housetraining on the right foot by teaching your dog that you prefer her to eliminate outside. Designate a potty area in your backyard (if you have one) or in the street in front of your home and take your dog to it as soon as you arrive

Don't Overuse the Crate

A crate serves well as a dog's overnight bed, but you should not leave the dog in her crate for more than an hour or two during the day. Throughout the day, she needs to play and exercise. She is likely to want to drink some water and will undoubtedly eliminate. Confining your dog all day will give her no option but to soil her crate. This is not just unpleasant for you and the dog, but it reinforces bad cleanliness habits. And crating a pup for the whole day is abusive. Don't do it.

home. Let her sniff a bit and, when she squats to go, give the action a name: "potty" or "do it" or anything else you won't be embarrassed to say in public. Eventually your dog will associate that word with the act and will eliminate on command. When she's finished, praise her with "good potty!"

That first day, take your puppy out to the potty area frequently. Although she may not eliminate every time, you are establishing a routine: You take her to her spot, ask her to eliminate, and praise her when she does.

Just before bedtime, take your dog to her potty area once more. Stand by and wait until she produces. Do not put your dog to bed for the night until she has eliminated. Be patient and calm. This is not the time to play with or excite your dog. If she's too excited, a pup not only won't eliminate, she probably won't want to sleep either.

Most dogs, even young ones, will not soil their beds if they can avoid it. For this reason, a sleeping crate can be a tremendous help during housetraining. Being crated at night can help a dog develop the muscles that control elimination. So after your dog has emptied out, put her to bed in her crate.

A good place to put your dog's sleeping crate is near your own bed. Dogs are pack animals, so they feel safer sleeping with others in a common area. In your bedroom, the pup will be near you and you'll be close enough to hear when she wakes during the night and needs to eliminate.

Pups under 4 months old often are not able to hold their urine all night. If your puppy has settled down to sleep but awakens and fusses a few hours later, she probably needs to go out. For the best housetraining progress, take your pup to her elimination area whenever she needs to go, even in the wee hours of the morning.

Your dog's crate will be an important housetraining tool.

Your pup may soil in her crate if you ignore her late night urgency. It's unfair to let this happen, and it sends the wrong message about your expectations for cleanliness. Resign yourself to this midnight outing and just get up and take the pup out. Your pup will outgrow this need soon and will learn in the process that she can count on you, and you'll wake happily each morning to a clean dog.

The next morning, the very first order of business is to take your pup out to eliminate. Don't forget to take her to her special potty spot, ask her to eliminate, and then praise her when she does. After your pup empties out in the morning, give her breakfast, and then take her to her potty area again. After that, she shouldn't need to eliminate again right away, so you can allow her some free playtime. Keep an eye on the pup though, because when she pauses in play she may need to go potty. Take her to the right spot, give the command, and praise if she produces.

Confine Your Pup

A pup or dog who has not finished housetraining should *never* be allowed the run of the house unattended. A new dog (especially a puppy) with unlimited access to your house will make her own choices about where to eliminate. Vigilance during your new dog's first few weeks in your home will pay big dividends. Every potty mistake delays housetraining progress; every success speeds it along.

Prevent problems by setting up a controlled environment for your new pet. A good place for a puppy corral is often the kitchen. Kitchens almost always have waterproof or easily cleaned floors, which is a distinct asset with leaky pups. A bathroom, laundry room, or enclosed porch could be used for a puppy corral, but the kitchen is generally the best location. Kitchens are a meeting place and a hub of activity for many families, and a puppy will learn better manners when she is socialized thoroughly with family, friends, and nice strangers.

The way you structure your pup's corral area is very important. Her bed, food, and water should be at the opposite end of the corral from the potty area. When you first get your pup, spread newspaper over the rest of the floor of her playpen corral. Lay the papers at least four pages thick and be sure to overlap the edges. As you note the pup's progress, you can remove the papers nearest the sleeping and eating corner. Gradually decrease the size of the papered area until only the end where you want the pup to eliminate is covered. If you will be training your dog to eliminate outside, place newspaper at the end of the corral that is closest to the door that leads outdoors. That way as she moves away from the clean area to the papered area, the pup will also form the habit of heading toward the door to go out.

Maintain a scent marker for the pup's potty area by reserving a small soiled piece of paper when you clean up. Place this piece, with her scent of urine, under the top sheet of the clean papers you spread. This will cue your pup where to eliminate.

Most dog owners use a combination of indoor papers and outdoor elimination areas. When the pup is left by herself in the corral, she can potty on the ever-present newspaper. When you are available to take the pup outside, she can do her business in the outdoor spot. It is not difficult to switch a pup from indoor paper training to outdoor elimination. Owners of large pups often switch early, but potty papers are still useful if the pup spends time in her indoor corral while you're away. Use the papers as long as your pup needs them. If you come home and they haven't been soiled, you are ahead.

When setting up your pup's outdoor yard, put the lounging area as far away as possible from the potty area, just as with the indoor corral setup. People with large yards, for example, might leave a patch unmowed at the edge of the lawn to serve as the dog's elimination area. Other dog owners teach the dog to relieve herself in a designated corner of a deck or patio. For an apartment-dwelling city dog, the outdoor potty area might be a tiny balcony or the curb. Each dog owner has somewhat different expectations for their dog. Teach your dog to eliminate in a spot that suits your environment and lifestyle.

> **TIP**
>
> **Water**
>
> Make sure your dog has access to clean water at all times. Limiting the amount of water a dog drinks is not necessary for housetraining success and can be very dangerous. A dog needs water to digest food, to maintain a proper body temperature and proper blood volume, and to clean her system of toxins and wastes. A healthy dog will automatically drink the right amount. Do not restrict water intake. Controlling your dog's access to water is not the key to housetraining her; controlling her access to everything else in your home is.

Take your pup to her outdoor potty place frequently throughout the day. Keep her leashed so she won't just wander around.

Be sure to pick up droppings in your yard at least once a day. Dogs have a natural desire to stay far away from their own excrement, and if too many piles litter the ground, your dog won't want to walk through it and will start eliminating elsewhere. Leave just one small piece of feces in the potty area to remind your dog where the right spot is located.

To help a pup adapt to the change from indoors to outdoors, take one of her potty papers outside to the new elimination area. Let the pup stand on the paper when she goes potty outdoors. Each day for four days, reduce the size of the paper by half. By the fifth day, the pup, having used a smaller and smaller piece of paper to stand on, will probably just go to that spot and eliminate.

Take your pup to her outdoor potty place frequently throughout the day. A puppy can hold her urine for only about as many hours as her age in months, and will move her bowels as many times a day as she eats. So a 2-month-old pup will urinate about every two hours, while at 4 months she can manage about four hours between piddles. Pups vary somewhat in their rate of development, so this is not a hard and fast rule. It does, however, present a realistic idea of how long a pup can be left without access to a potty place. Past 4 months, her potty trips will be less frequent.

When you take the dog outdoors to her spot, keep her leashed so that she won't wander away. Stand quietly and let her sniff around in the designated area.

If your pup starts to leave before she has eliminated, gently lead her back and remind her to go. If your pup sniffs at the spot, praise her calmly, say the command word, and just wait. If she produces, praise serenely, then give her time to sniff around a little more. She may not be finished, so give her time to go again before allowing her to play and explore her new home.

If you find yourself waiting more than five minutes for your dog to potty, take her back inside. Watch your pup carefully for twenty minutes, not giving her any opportunity to slip away to eliminate unnoticed. If you are too busy to watch the pup, put her in her crate. After twenty minutes, take her to the outdoor potty spot again and tell her what to do. If you're unsuccessful after five minutes, crate the dog again. Give her another chance to eliminate in fifteen or twenty minutes. Eventually, she will have to go.

Watch Your Pup

Be vigilant and don't let the pup make a mistake in the house. Each time you successfully anticipate elimination and take your pup to the potty spot, you'll move a step closer to your goal. Stay aware of your puppy's needs. If you ignore the pup, she will make mistakes and you'll be cleaning up more messes.

Keep a chart of your new dog's elimination behavior for the first three or four days. Jot down what times she eats, sleeps, and eliminates. After several days a pattern will emerge that can help you determine your pup's body rhythms. Most dogs tend to eliminate at fairly regular intervals. Once you know your new dog's natural rhythms, you'll be able to anticipate her needs and schedule appropriate potty outings.

Understanding the meanings of your dog's postures can also help you win the battle of the puddle. When your dog is getting ready to eliminate, she will display a specific set of postures. The sooner you can learn to read these signals, the cleaner your floor will stay.

A young puppy who feels the urge to eliminate may start to sniff the ground and walk in a circle. If the pup is very young, she may simply squat and go. All young puppies, male or female, squat to urinate. If you are housetraining a

You can't mistake the postures of a dog who has to go.

pup under 4 months of age, regardless of sex, watch for the beginnings of a squat as the signal to rush the pup to the potty area.

When a puppy is getting ready to defecate, she may run urgently back and forth or turn in a circle while sniffing or starting to squat. If defecation is imminent, the pup's anus may protrude or open slightly. When she starts to go, the pup will squat and hunch her back, her tail sticking straight out behind. There is no mistaking this posture; nothing else looks like this. If your pup takes this position, take her to her potty area. Hurry! You may have to carry her to get there in time.

A young puppy won't have much time between feeling the urge and actually eliminating, so you'll have to be quick to note her postural clues and intercept your pup in time. Pups from 3 to 6 months have a few seconds more between the urge and the act than younger ones do. The older your pup, the more time you'll have to get her to the potty area after she begins the posture signals that alert you to her need.

Accidents Happen

If you see your pup about to eliminate somewhere other than the designated area, interrupt her immediately. Say "wait, wait, wait!" or clap your hands loudly to startle her into stopping. Carry the pup, if she's still small enough, or take her collar and lead her to the correct area. Once your dog is in the potty area, give her the command to eliminate. Use a friendly voice for the command, then wait patiently for her to produce. The pup may be tense because you've just startled her and may have to relax a bit before she's able to eliminate. When she does her job, include the command word in the praise you give ("good potty").

The old-fashioned way of housetraining involved punishing a dog's mistakes even before she knew what she was supposed to do. Puppies were punished for breaking rules they didn't understand about functions they couldn't control. This was not fair. While your dog is new to housetraining, there is no need or excuse for punishing her mistakes. Your job is to take the dog to the potty area just before she needs to go, especially with pups under 3 months old. If you aren't watching your pup closely enough and she has an accident, don't punish the puppy for your failure to anticipate her needs. It's not the pup's fault; it's yours.

In any case, punishment is not an effective tool for housetraining most dogs. Many will react to punishment by hiding puddles and feces where you won't find them right away (like behind the couch or under the desk). This eventually may lead to punishment after the fact, which leads to more hiding, and so on.

Instead of punishing for mistakes, stay a step ahead of potty accidents by learning to anticipate your pup's needs. Accompany your dog to the designated potty area when she needs to go. Tell her what you want her to do and praise her

A baby puppy does not have the physical ability to control her bladder and bowels for very long. Please don't expect more from your dog than she can do.

when she goes. This will work wonders. Punishment won't be necessary if you are a good teacher.

What happens if you come upon a mess after the fact? Some trainers say a dog can't remember having eliminated, even a few moments after she has done so. This is not true. The fact is that urine and feces carry a dog's unique scent, which she (and every other dog) can instantly recognize. So, if you happen upon a potty mistake after the fact you can still use it to teach your dog.

But remember, no punishment! Spanking, hitting, shaking, or scaring a puppy for having a housetraining accident is confusing and counterproductive. Spend your energy instead on positive forms of teaching.

Take your pup and a paper towel to the mess. Point to the urine or feces and calmly tell your puppy, "no potty here." Then scoop or sop up the accident with the paper towel. Take the evidence and the pup to the approved potty area. Drop the mess on the ground and tell the dog, "good potty here," as if she had done the deed in the right place. If your pup sniffs at the evidence, praise her calmly. If the accident happened very recently your dog may not have to go yet, but wait with her a few minutes anyway. If she eliminates, praise her. Afterwards, go finish cleaning up the mess.

Soon the puppy will understand that there is a place where you are pleased about elimination and other places where you are not. Praising for elimination in the approved place will help your pup remember the rules.

Scheduling Basics

With a new puppy in the home, don't be surprised if your rising time is suddenly a little earlier than you've been accustomed to. Puppies have earned a reputation as very early risers. When your pup wakes you at the crack of dawn, you will have to get up and take her to her elimination spot. Be patient. When your dog is an adult, she may enjoy sleeping in as much as you do.

At the end of the chapter, you'll find a typical housetraining schedule for puppies aged 10 weeks to 6 months. (To find schedules for younger and older pups, and for adult dogs, visit this book's companion web site.) It's fine to adjust the rising times when using this schedule, but you should not adjust the intervals between feedings and potty outings unless your pup's behavior justifies a change. Your puppy can only meet your expectations in housetraining if you help her learn the rules.

The schedule for puppies is devised with the assumption that someone will be home most of the time with the pup. That would be the best scenario, of course, but is not always possible. You may be able to ease the problems of a latchkey pup by having a neighbor or friend look in on the pup at noon and take her to eliminate. A better solution might be hiring a pet sitter to drop by midday. A professional pet sitter will be knowledgeable about companion animals and can give your pup high-quality care and socialization. Some can even

Housetraining may seem like it takes up all your time at first. But as your dog gets older, she will learn to control herself and you'll be able to schedule fewer walks.

help train your pup in both potty manners and basic obedience. Ask your veterinarian and your dog-owning friends to recommend a good pet sitter.

If you must leave your pup alone during her early housetraining period, be sure to cover the entire floor of her corral with thick layers of overlapping newspaper. If you come home to messes in the puppy corral, just clean them up. Be patient—she's still a baby.

Use this schedule (and the ones on the companion web site) as a basic plan to help prevent housetraining accidents. Meanwhile, use your own powers of observation to discover how to best modify the basic schedule to fit your dog's unique needs. Each dog is an individual and will have her own rhythms, and each dog is reliable at a different age.

Schedule for Pups 10 Weeks to 6 Months

7:00 a.m.	Get up and take the puppy from her sleeping crate to her potty spot.
7:15	Clean up last night's messes, if any.
7:30	Food and fresh water.
7:45	Pick up the food bowl. Take the pup to her potty spot; wait and praise.
8:00	The pup plays around your feet while you have your breakfast.
9:00	Potty break (younger pups may not be able to wait this long).
9:15	Play and obedience practice.
10:00	Potty break.
10:15	The puppy is in her corral with safe toys to chew and play with.
11:30	Potty break (younger pups may not be able to wait this long).
11:45	Food and fresh water.
12:00 p.m.	Pick up the food bowl and take the pup to her potty spot.
12:15	The puppy is in her corral with safe toys to chew and play with.
1:00	Potty break (younger pups may not be able to wait this long).

continues

Schedule for Pups 10 Weeks to 6 Months *(continued)*

1:15	Put the pup on a leash and take her around the house with you.
3:30	Potty break (younger pups may not be able to wait this long).
3:45	Put the pup in her corral with safe toys and chews for solitary play and/or a nap.
4:45	Potty break.
5:00	Food and fresh water.
5:15	Potty break.
5:30	The pup may play nearby (either leashed or in her corral) while you prepare your evening meal.
7:00	Potty break.
7:15	Leashed or closely watched, the pup may play and socialize with family and visitors.
9:15	Potty break (younger pups may not be able to wait this long).
10:45	Last chance to potty.
11:00	Put the pup to bed in her crate for the night.

Appendix

Learning More About Your Boston Terrier

Some Good Books

Baker, Donna S., and Paul Hiller, *Boston Terrier Collectibles*, Schiffer Publishing, 2003.

Lee, Muriel, *The Official Book of the Boston Terrier*, TFH Publications, 1998.

Staley, Beverly, and Michael Staley, *The Boston Terrier: An American Original*, Howell Book House, 1995.

Care and Health

Arden, Darlene, *The Angell Memorial Animal Hospital Book of Wellness & Preventive Care for Dogs*, McGraw-Hill, 2002.

Arden, Darlene, *Small Dogs, Big Hearts: A Guide to Caring for Your Little Dog*, Howell Book House, 2006.

Bamberger, Michelle, DVM, *Help! The Quick Guide to First Aid for Your Dog*, Howell Book House, 1995.

Messonnier, Shawn, DVM, *Natural Health Bible for Dogs & Cats: Your A-Z Guide to Over 200 Conditions, Herbs, Vitamins, and Supplements*, Three Rivers Press, 2001.

Training

Kalstone, Shirlee, *How to Housebreak Your Dog in Seven Days*, Revised Edition, Bantam Books, 2004.

McConnell, Patricia, *The Other End of the Leash*, Ballantine Books, 2003.

Smith, Cheryl S., *The Rosetta Bone*, Howell Book House, 2004.

Canine Activities

Cecil, Barbara, and Gerianne Darnell, *Competitive Obedience Training for the Small Dog*, T9E Publishing, 1994.

Davis, Kathy Diamond, *Therapy Dogs: Training Your Dog to Help Others*, 2nd Edition, Dogwise Publications, 2002.

Simmons-Moake, Jane, *Agility Training: The Fun Sport for All Dogs*, Howell Book House, 1991.

Smith, Cheryl S., *The Absolute Beginner's Guide to Showing Your Dog*, Three Rivers Press, 2001.

Volhard, Jack and Wendy, *The Canine Good Citizen: Every Dog Can Be One*, 2nd Edition, Howell Book House, 1997.

Clubs and Registries

American Kennel Club (AKC)
260 Madison Ave.
New York, NY 10016
www.akc.org
The American Kennel Club can provide you with a list of breed and canine sport clubs in your area.

Boston Terrier Club of America, Inc. (BTCA)
3878 Banks Rd.
Cincinatti, OH 45245
www.btca.org
The Boston Terrier Club of America Health Committee publishes *The Boston Terrier Puppy Owners Handbook*. Write to 222 Walnut Dr., Pendleton, KY 4055-7731, or e-mail ewieland@stites.com to purchase the book, which costs $10.

Canadian Kennel Club (CKC)
89 Skyway Ave.
Etobicoke, Ontario
Canada M9W 6R4
(800) 250-8040 or (416) 675-5511
www.ckc.ca

United Kennel Club (UKC)
100 E. Kilgore Rd.
Kalamazoo, MI 49001-5598
(616) 343-9020
www.ukcdogs.com

Magazines

AKC Gazette
AKC Family Dog
260 Madison Ave.
New York, NY 10016
(212) 696-8200
www.akc.org

The Bark
2810 8th St.
Berkeley, CA 94710
(510) 704-0827

The Boston Quarterly
Hoflin Publishing Inc.
4401 Zephyr St.
Wheat Ridge, CO 80033
www.hoflin.com/Magazines/
Magazines.html

Dog Fancy
P.O. Box 37185
Boone, IA 50037-0185
(800) 896-4939
www.dogfancy.com

Dogs in Canada
Apex Publishing Limited
89 Skyway Ave., Suite 200
Etobicoke, Ontario
M9W 6R4, Canada
(416) 798-9778
subscriptionweb@dogsincanada.com

DogWorld
P.O. Box 37185
Boone, IA 50037-0185
(800) 896-4939
www.dogworldmag.com

Web Sites

Activities

Canine Freestyle Federation
www.canine-freestyle.com
This site is devoted to canine freestyle—dancing with your dog. There's information about freestyle events, tips, and even music to choose!

Delta Society
www.deltasociety.org
The Delta Society promotes the human–animal bond through pet-assisted therapy and other programs.

General Information

American Society for the Prevention of Cruelty to Animals

www.aspca.org

Features humane education and advocacy information, with a link to the ASPCA Poison Control Center.

Infodog

www.infodog.com

This is a good site for locating AKC-licensed dog shows and obedience or agility trials in your area. It also has links to rescue organizations nationwide.

Travel

Dog Friendly

www.dogfriendly.com

Information about traveling with dogs, including guidebooks.

Travel Dog

www.traveldog.com

Lots of information on where you and your dog will be welcome when you travel.

Veterinary Organizations

American Animal Hospital Association

www.healthypet.com

Information on pet health and ownership trends.

American Holistic Veterinary Medicine Association

www.ahvma.org

Information on holistic care, and a search feature to help you find practitioners in your area.

American Veterinary Medical Association

www.avma.org

The latest veterinary medical news.

Index